Correcting Deficiencies in the Basic Skills

(Help for the Frustrated Teacher)

Grades 4 - 8

Nettie Whitney Bailey

ISBN 0-7596-5608-8 (Electronic)
ISBN 0-7596-5609-6 (Softcover)

This book is printed on acid free paper.

1stBooks – rev. 06/13/02

Introduction . . .

Research* shows that there are many children who are not functioning at grade level. In many cases, the result is frustrated teachers; frustrated because you are working hard but not seeing the improvement in your students that you desire.

Children are to *learn to read* from Headstart through third grade. From grade four throughout their years in school, they are to *read to learn.*

When students have not mastered all the steps in the reading process, it becomes your responsibility to recognize the deficiencies, address them when they appear in *any subject*, give the students opportunities to learn them, practice them, and, in time, master them. Certainly this will impact the speed that the curriculum dictates. My question -- "What is accomplished if the students understand little or nothing of what is being presented in class or given as homework in order 'to keep pace'?" Little or nothing! Your question -- "How can I meet the demands of the prescribed curriculum *and* address the deficiencies?" Review, select, and use the material in this volume.

Tutoring children enrolled in public and private schools during the past decade has confirmed what research* has shown. As I identified their deficiencies, I created exercises to give practice in them, and helped the children learn to thoughtfully take the necessary steps to right answers rather than guess, they were able to improve their scores on achievement tests such as the Iowa Test of Basic Skills.

The same deficiencies were present, tutee after tutee after tutee. The exercises included in this volume address those deficiencies. If you apply the information included, identify the deficiencies, and use the exercises (make copies as needed) in conjunction with the prescribed curriculum, you will see improvement in your students. If there is little or no support from home, there will be limited improvement, but improvement just the same. If there is more support from home -- parents/guardians making sure homework assignments are done thoughtfully and neatly -- there will be more improvement.

Use your creativity to modify your grade-level materials so that they meet the needs of your students. Do all you can do while the students are with you and you will have done a good job, deserving to be called "teacher".

*Mullis, I. V. S., Campbell, J. R., & Farstrup, A. E., (1993)

NAEP 1992 reading report card for the nation and the states:

Data from the national and trial state assessments. Washington, D. C. : U. S. Dept. Of Education, National Center for Educational Statistics.

Notes about the author . . .

I met Mrs. Bailey while Principal at Marshall High School in Chicago, Illinois. At that time, she and her husband were active as parents to a child for whom they were providing foster care. I was impressed with her community concern and involvement. After becoming District Superintendent I had the pleasure of working with her as she functioned within Beidler Elementary School as reading resource teacher in the Intensive Reading Improvement Program. This position required Mrs. Bailey to interact with teachers locally and city wide.

I have respect for Mrs. Bailey as an educator extraordinaire. She is able to function effectively from the position of administrator as well as classroom teacher. With these assurances, the information that she has chosen to provide is second to none. Her personality allows her to be sensitive to the students who will be the recipients of these activities as well as the teachers who will utilize this much needed tool.

I congratulate her and applaud this effort. I expect nothing but widespread praise from the educational community.

Dr. Robert A. Saddler
Retired Deputy Superintendent
Chicago Public Schools

Dedication . . .

Many have contributed in a variety of ways to the completion of this volume.

Evangelist Robbie Foster provided my daily care and performed every task related to this book that my legs would not allow me to do. Robbie is my friend. Thank you.

Several teachers shared some of their experiences which further highlighted the need for the tools I've included. Thank you!

My many calls for help were answered by computer literate friends and family members who lovingly reminded me that computers do only what they are told to do. Thank you!

I thank God, the Ultimate Arranger, Who gave me the idea and served as the overseer for the project. He is
awesomeomnimerfulsalousexemirafaily!

I dedicate this book to Mrs. Geraldine Moore, Principal of Beidler Elementary School on the westside of Chicago, and to the parents who have trusted me to work with their precious children. Thank you!

The children. The children. The children. The children I tutored at Beidler and in my home identified, through their need, the skills other students also need. They never stopped trying to improve their performance as they used the practice sheets I created for them. Those sheets comprise the Appendix. The children never lost their desire to earn better grades in spite of repeated failures in their classrooms. They never gave up on their ability. I never gave up on them.

To God be the glory!

Acknowledgments . . .

All of the students I've worked with needed to understand that they didn't have to guess. They needed lots of direction and practice on how to think, how to take logical steps to find correct answers. In addition to the practice sheets I created, each student I tutored in my home worked in the Continental Press publication, *Reading-Thinking Skills*, which contributed greatly to the success they experienced when they took the end-of-the-year achievement test at their schools.

I referred to the books listed below to check the accuracy of some of the definitions I included.

The Merriam-Webster Dictionary
Published by Pocket Books
New York, 1974

Scott, Foresman Advanced Dictionary
E. L. Thorndike/Clarence L. Barnhart
Scott, Foresman and Company
1988

Silver Burdett English
Nancy Nickell Ragno, Marian Davies Toth
Betty G. Gray
Silver Burdett Company
Morristown, N. J., 1987

Contents...

Children Learn What They Live

When your students live with criticism,
They learn to condemn.
When they live with hostility,
They learn to fight.
When your students live with ridicule,
They learn to be shy.
When they live with jealousy,
They learn to feel guilty.
When your students live with tolerance,
They learn to be patient.
When they live with encouragement,
They learn confidence.
When your students live with praise,
They learn to appreciate.
When they live with fairness,
They learn justice.
When your students live with security,
They learn to have faith.
When they live with approval,
They learn to like themselves.
When your students live with acceptance and friendship,
Then learn to find love in the world.

Adaptation
Author unknown

Nettie Whitney Bailey

Parents -- the First Teachers

Contact parents on a regular basis. Share the following to encourage them. You have to deal with the negative attitudes of some of their children *only* five hours a day. The parents have to deal with them *all the rest of the time.*

COOK, JANITOR, NURSE,
FIGHT-STOPPER, MAID, AND PLUMBER,
LAUNDRESS, SEAMSTRESS, COUNSELOR,
BABY-SITTER, PAINTER, AND CARPENTER,
ELECTRICIAN, SHOPPER, GARDENER,
TOY-FIXER, TEAR-WIPER, AND DISH-WASHER.
AND PARENTS ARE THE FIRST TEACHERS.

YOU TEACH YOUR CHILDREN HOW TO LAUGH,
YOU HELP THEM WHEN THEY CRY.
YOU TEACH THEM HOW TO LISTEN,
TO ASK YOU "HOW?" AND "WHY?"

YOU TEACH THEM HOW TO LIKE AND LOVE,
AND SOMETIMES HOW TO HATE.
IF YOU DON'T TEACH THEM WHILE THEY'RE YOUNG,
YOUR CHILDREN WILL NOT WAIT.

YOU TEACH THEM HOW TO DRESS THEMSELVES,
THEIR SHOES TO TIE AND BUCKLE.
YOU TEACH THEM HOW TO COMB THEIR HAIR,
HOW TO WASH CLEAN AND NOT MISS A KNUCKLE.

YOU TEACH THEM HOW TO WALK AND TALK,
YOU TEACH THEM HOW TO PLAY.
YOU TEACH THEM UP, DOWN, LEFT, AND RIGHT,
COLORS, NUMBERS, AND THEIR NAMES TO SAY.

THERE ARE SO MANY THINGS YOU TEACH THEM,
I CANNOT LIST THEM ALL.
SCHOOL TEACHERS MUST CERTAINLY DO THEIR PART
BUT, PARENTS, YOU'RE TEACHERS TOO!
SO STAND UP, PROUD AND TALL!

Adaptation Author Unknown

PLEDGES OF INTEGRITY can be used each morning and whenever there are discussions about behavior.

PLEDGES OF INTEGRITY

(Integrity -- doing the right thing)

We are children of integrity.
We will be honest at all times.
We will do the right thing at home.
We will do the right thing at school.
We will do the right thing at all times.

I am a girl of integrity.
I will be honest at all times.
I will do the right thing at home.
I will do the right thing at school.
I will do the right thing at all times.

I am a boy of integrity.
I will be honest at all times.
I will do the right thing at home.
I will do the right thing at school.
I will do the right thing at all times.

Adaptation
Mrs. Yvonne Brown, Teacher Assistant
John Harvard Elementary School
Chicago, IL

AREAS OF POSSIBLE DEFICIENCIES THAT NEED TO BE ADDRESSED

Create bulletin boards with whatever portion(s) of this information you have determined that the students need to learn, review, or practice. See the Appendix for exercises that can assess and/or give practice in these areas.

PARTS OF A BOOK
Title Page --
Can the students identify the author? illustrator? publisher? place of publication? copyright date?

Table of Contents --
Do the students know where it is, when to use it, and why?
Can the students determine the number of pages in each selection/chapter?

Glossary --
Do the students know where it is, when to use it, and why?

Index --
Do the students know where it is, when to use it, and why?

DICTIONARY

Can the students use the guide words? the Pronunciation Key?
Can the students understand the abbreviations and punctuation?
Do the students know how to choose the correct meaning?

THESAURUS

Do the students know what it is, when to use it, and why?

SENTENCES

Do the students know the difference between a sentence and a line in a selection? how paragraphs are identified? the kinds of words that are capitalized? when to use the various punctuation marks?

VOCABULARY

Can the students recognize, spell, use, and alphabetize the Dolch words?

Can the students read, understand, form, and use contractions? possessives? compound words?

Can the students recognize, spell, and use homonyms and words with multiple meanings?

Can the students recognize, read, and use the parts of speech?

Can the students read and understand specific vocabulary for each subject being taught? [Language Arts, (Reading, Spelling, English, Handwriting, Creative Writing), Math, Science, Social Science, Fine Arts, Health and Safety]

If you did not take an undergrad course in the teaching of reading, or have not used a phonetically based basal reading series, all the bits and pieces that students need to unlock unknown words and understand what they read may escape your notice. Read and digest these "bits and pieces" so you can help your students learn to use them.

Tell students unfamiliar or unknown words and you help them during that lesson. Teach them how to unlock unfamiliar or unknown words and you help them for the rest of their lives.

WORD ATTACK SKILLS

PHONICS

Can the student use the following to unlock unfamiliar words?

A. Initial, middle, final consonants/consonant clusters. When these letters appear in a word, each is sounded:

> bl, cl, fl, gl pl, sl, br, cr, dr, fr, gr, pr, tr,
>
> sc sk, sl, sm, sn, sp, st, sw, scr, spl,
>
> spr, str,

When these letters appear in a word, they represent one sound:

ch, sh, gh, ph, th

B. Short vowel sounds:

> **a**t, **e**gg, br**ea**d, **i**t, **o**dd, **u**p, r**ou**gh, g**y**m

Schwa sound -- Each vowel can have the sound of the short "u"

> as in **u**p -- **a**lone--eas**i**ly--dung**e**on--cymb**a**l--tass**e**l-
>
> g**i**raffe, gall**o**n,

C. Long vowel sounds are the same as the names of the vowels and can be spelled a number of ways:

> **A** **a**te--pl**ay**--th**ey**--r**ai**n--n**ei**ghbor--v**ei**l--st**ea**k--g**au**ge
>
> **E** **e**qual--th**e**me--m**ee**t--s**ea**t--n**ie**ce--p**eo**ple--k**ey**-- happ**y** dec**ei**ve--machine
>
> **I** **i**ce--p**ie**--**ai**sle--cr**y**--**eye**--h**ei**ght
>
> **O** **o**h--t**o**te--b**oa**t--s**ew**--r**ow**--s**ou**l--t**oe**
>
> **U** **u**se--c**u**te--f**ew**--b**eau**tiful--f**eu**d--q**ueue**

D. Vowel combinations -- b**oi**l--t**oy**--c**au**ght--r**aw**--b**ou**ght,

book--b**oo**t--n**ew**--h**ou**se--c**ow**

E. Silent letters--**gh**ost--**w**ring--**k**nee--**g**nat--**gu**ess--bu**y**--clim**b**

7

sign--scratch--ridge--walk

F. Syllables -- each syllable has only one vowel sound which can be represented by one or more letters.

STRUCTURAL ANALYSIS

[ROOT WORDS AND AFFIXES (one or more letters added to the beginning or end of a root word)]

A. Prefixes -- one or more letters added to the beginning of a root word that changes the meaning or forms another word.

un-, in-, im-, dis-, mis- (not)

Examples: untie, **in**decent, **im**material, **dis**respect, **mis**understand

re- (again) pre- (before)

Examples: rewrite, **re**turn, **re**new, **pre**paid

B. Suffixes -- one or more letters added to the end of a root word that changes (1) the number (singular to plural), (2) the tense (to present or past), or (3) the function (from one part of speech to another).

1. **-s, -es**

Examples: boy**s**, store**s**, box**es**, dish**es**

-ing, -ed

Example: listen**ing**, listen**ed**; remember**ing**, remember**ed**

2. **-ful, -ous (full of)**

Examples: wonder**ful,** mountain**ous**

-less (without)

Examples: shoe**less**, penni**less**,

-or, -er (one that does a specific thing)

Examples: calculat**or**, teach**er**

-ion (the act, result, or condition of an action; changes verbs to nouns)

Examples: attract to attrac**tion**

abbreviate to abbrevia**tion**

adopt to adop**tion**

COMPREHENSION

Before reading the selection, are the students able to tell what they think the selection might be about and/or what they already know and what they would like to know about the subject?

- When given a purpose for reading small sections at a time, can they locate information you tell them to find as they read? Can they discuss Who?, What?, When?, Where? (factual) questions? Can they identify the main character, other characters, where and when the selection takes place, what the characters do, the sequence of events, etc.?

- Can the students discuss How? and Why? (inferential and evaluative) questions? Can they identify the main idea (what the whole story is about) and identify details that support the main idea? Can they discuss why the characters do what they do, how the characters feel about the circumstances and each other? Can they identify the main character's problem and how it is solved? Can they discuss what they think will happen next and tell the difference between fact and opinion? Can they suggest why the author wrote the selection, how he/she feels about the subject, and how he/she wants the reader to feel about the subject, etc.?

- Can the students discuss what they learned? Are they motivated to learn more about the subject?

- Can the students tell the story in their words?

ALL-SUBJECT LESSON PLAN TO ADDRESS DEFICIENCIES

I. Title/Picture -- What do students think the selection/chapter will be about?

Have them share similar personal experiences or prior knowledge of the topic.

II. Teach and review vocabulary. ***THERE WILL BE LITTLE OR NO COMPREHENSION IF THIS IS NOT DONE***.

   Time-saving hint:
   Assign new vocabulary as homework the evening before the lesson is to be introduced. Have students alphabetize the words, and/or use the glossary or the dictionary to define the words. If the students are to use the dictionary, be sure to identify the part of speech for each word as it is used in the selection. Never assume that students know how to do anything you assign. Always review the steps they need to take to complete the assignment with examples.

   A. Pronunciation -- Tell them that they know all the sounds of all of the letters because they talk all the time, and talk is just putting the sounds of letters together and saying words.

      1) Guide them through printed pronunciations that are often given with difficult words, often proper names.

      2) Have the students identify and pronounce smaller recognizable words, prefixes, and suffixes within the words.

      3) Help them divide words into syllables. Tell them the vowel ***sound*** in each syllable and have them blend the sounds by pronouncing each syllable in order.

    4) Tell them that they do not have to spend a lot of time trying to pronounce proper nouns. Tell them to use the context to figure out if it is the name of a person, a place, or a thing.

B. Meanings

    1) Help the students recognize the meanings of unfamiliar words that are provided within a selection/chapter as indicated by:

      a. the clue word "or" which precedes the definition.

      b. commas or parenthesis which set apart or enclose the definition.

    2) Call their attention to other words in the sentence that will help them figure out the meaning.

    3) Write or recite sentences using new vocabulary.

III. Time to read.

Give a **purpose** for reading (Tell the students what you want them to find out, paragraph by paragraph or page by page.)

Remember, oral reading most often tends to limit comprehension. The students' focus is on saying the words correctly and not meaning. Since they usually like to read aloud, ask the listening students to answer the questions.

Read to the students. Sometimes have the students read along. Sometimes, tell them to follow along as you read, and when you stop, tell them to read the next word, preferably one of the new words. Tell them to pay close attention so they can know if you are pausing for proper phrasing or for a comma, stopping for a period, or stopping for them to read the next word.

Have good readers and poorer readers read aloud together.

Ask literal, inferential, and evaluative questions. (See page 10.)

Ask more inferential and evaluative questions because these are the questions that most children miss on achievement tests such as the Iowa Test of Basic Skills.

ADDITIONAL CONTENT AREA READING TIPS

What do the students already know? Why is the lesson important? What do they want/need to find out? How will/can it help them?

Teach the use of the page(s) that precede practice exercises and practice problems. When the students try to do the homework assignment and realize they have forgotten how to do it, they can refer to these pages.

Use the language of the subject you are teaching on a daily basis, especially math. If the students have not learned the vocabulary for that subject previously, use the new terms interchangeably with the terms they are accustomed to using.

Examples: answer/sum/difference/product/quotient; take away/subtract; pluses/addition; dividend/number inside the box; top of the map/north; etc.

HERE IS A TIP OF IMMEASURABLE VALUE:

Have the students solve math problems on the chalkboard and explain how they solved them using math language.

CONSONANT/VOWEL SOUNDS

Memory Game.

The first person chooses a sentence and fills in the blank with a word that begins with "a". The next person repeats the sentence and fills in the blank with the "a" word and gives a word that begins with "b", etc. throughout the alphabet.

Variation. Read one of the sentences aloud and ask a student to fill the blank with any word they choose, then identify the ending and/or middle consonant(s) and/or vowel(s).

I went to the grocery store and bought _____.

I went to the zoo and saw _____.

I went to the Jewel/K-Mart/Toys-R-Us and bought_____.

I went to the park and saw_____.

I know a person whose name is _____.

I know a job/profession/career that begins with _____.

I know the name of a place that begins with_____.

I know the name of a country/state/city that begins with _____.

I know the name of a thing that begins with_____.

I know a verb that begins with _____.

I know an adjective that begins with _____.

(Use other parts of speech also.)

SOUND BLENDING

Choose a category. Sound out the name of a person, a place, or a thing. Have the students guess the name/noun. Have them repeat it and/or sound out a noun of their choice.

girls'/ boys' names	L-ee	C-a-th-y	B-i-ll	J-a-m-es
places to eat		M-a-c-D-o-n-a-l-d-s	k-i-t-ch-e-n	

14

places to play	p-a-r-k	ou-t-s-i-d
things in the room	t-a-b-l	w-i-n-d-ow
animals	c-a-t	g-i -r-a-ff
fruit	a-pp-l	g-r-a-p
vegetables	c-a-rr-o-t-s	g-r-ee-n b-ea-n-s

BOOK SENSE

(VOCABULARY AND USE)

Looking at the textbooks in their desks, have the students choose one and identify each part of it that is listed in Group A and describe its function. Obtain copies of the reference materials not usually available in the classroom (Group B) and discuss how and why each is used. Have them use each of the words in Groups A and B in a sentence and explain how they have used or will use it.

GROUP A

Textbook
Cover
Spine
Title page
(Author, Illustrator, Publisher, Place of publication, Copyright date)
Table of Contents
Index
Gazetteer
Glossary

GROUP B

Almanac
Atlas
Dictionary (guide words, entry words, pronunciation key, meanings/definitions, abbreviations, superscripts)
Encyclopedia
Thesaurus (synonyms, antonyms)
Card catalog
Internet

PUNCTUATION

Suggested activities:

1. Have students look up each of the following marks of punctuation in the glossary in their English books or in the dictionary and write a description of when each is used.
2. Choose a fiction book. Find and copy sentences in which at least one of the marks is used.
3. Write sentences using at least one punctuation mark in each.
4. Write a paragraph and use all of the punctuation marks.

. period

? question mark

! exclamation mark

, comma

' apostrophe

" " quotation marks

; semicolon

: colon

( ) parenthesis

HOMEWORK ASSIGNMENTS FOR STUDENTS WHO CANNOT READ THE GRADE-LEVEL TEXT

(See the Appendix for homework assignments to assess or practice particular skills.)

MATH

Give daily practice on the number facts (If students cannot give answers to addition, subtraction, multiplication, and division facts as quickly as they respond to, "What is your name?", they need to practice!)

Give practice in place value -- reading and writing number names through trillions; underline digits in numerals and have the students identify their values.

LANGUAGE ARTS

Vocabulary -- Give words from the next lesson to be taught and have the students look them up in the dictionary. Tell them which definitions/meanings you want them to write by identifying the part of speech (noun, verb, etc). that is used in the selection. Have them use the thesaurus sometimes.

Give them practice in determining the accuracy of their choice by using the context. Have them replace the word in the context with the meaning they chose and see if it makes sense.

Have the students write sentences using the words they looked up in the dictionary or thesaurus.

Pronoun practice -- Using selections from their textbooks, identify pronouns and have the students identify their antecedents, the nouns they are replacing.

ALL SUBJECTS -- USE THE NEWSPAPER

1. Have the students write captions or stories for pictures taken from the newspaper.
2. Use headlines to clarify the concept of main idea.
3. Select several cartoons, cut them apart, and have the students put them back in order, giving them practice in sequencing.
4. Have the students choose an article from a week-end edition and report on it on Monday, using the 5 W's. (Who, What, When, Where, Why)
5. Have the students use the grocery store advertisements in the food section to plan a meal and figure out how much it will cost.
6. Use the graphs (bar, line, circle) to learn how to read or practice reading them.
7. Use the weather map to discuss social science and science.
8. Use political cartoons to work on literal and inferential comprehension.
9. Compare reports on the same incident from different newspapers.
10. Have the students watch the news on television. Compare one of the reports with the newspaper account.
11. Explain that newspaper reporters structure their text like an inverted or upside down equilateral triangle. The lead or first paragraph gives the most important details. Information of lesser and lesser importance follows.

Nettie Whitney Bailey

ONLY A TEACHER

You are a scholar, you are now more aware of the skills children must develop in order to read.

You are a diagnostician, you use as many tools and devices as necessary to determine and meet individual needs.

You are an accountant, you keep records of your children's progress while others are enjoying evenings of fun or relaxation.

You are a sociologist, you form many groups according to the needs of the children that you try to meet.

You are an interior decorator, you have lots of ideas and you make your room a neat, attractive, exciting center for learning.

You are a reservationist, scheduling the children's activities so that they are not late for their usual favorites -- lunch, gym, recess.

You are an instructor, you have lots of children to teach.

You are a judge and an informant with information and suggestions that the children and your fellow teachers can benefit from.

Only a teacher, you understand why you are beat, yet others will never realize what makes up your week.

Only you know what it's like to teach, to have the patience and fortitude to change children into students, individuals who want to learn and enjoy the process.

Only you can enjoy the benefits others never reap!

Adaptation
Author Unknown

APPENDIX

Language Arts

Mathematics

Social Science (Geography)

Answers

LANGUAGE ARTS WORKSHEETS

All About Me (I Am Special)

26 Reasons I, _____, Am Wonderful

Ladder of Success

Following Written Directions

Parts of a Textbook

Dictionary

Thesaurus

Sentences, Lines, & Paragraphs

Reading and Alphabetizing Dolch Words

Initial Sounds

Capitalization and Punctuation

Contractions 1

Contractions 2

Noun Markers (Articles)

Nouns

Common Nouns, Proper Nouns, Verbs, and Adjectives

Nouns, Verbs, & Adjectives 1

Nouns, Verbs, & Adjectives 2

Nouns, Pronouns, Verbs, and Adjectives

Multiple Meanings

Singular, Plural, and Possessive Nouns/Pronoun Contractions

Eight Parts of Speech

Pronoun Antecedents

Directed Reading Lesson (Emphasis: Pronoun Antecedents)

Homonyms 1

Homonyms 2

Subjects for Creative Writing (Narrative, Expository, Descriptive)

Subjects for Creative Writing (Persuasive)

Read-aloud Selection (Omar by Nettie Whitney Bailey)

MATHEMATICS WORKSHEETS

Math Language

Addition Facts 1

1A Addition/Subtraction Practice. .

Addition Facts 2

2A Addition/Subtraction Practice

Addition Facts 3

3A Addition/Subtraction Practice

Addition Facts 4

4A Addition/Subtraction Practice

Addition Facts 5

5A Addition/Subtraction Practice

Addition Facts 6

6A Addition/Subtraction Practice

Addition Table

Addition/Multiplication (0's)

Addition/Multiplication (1's)

Addition/Multiplication (2's)

Addition/Multiplication (3's)

Addition/Multiplication (4's)

Addition/Multiplication (5's)

Addition/Multiplication (6's)

Addition/Multiplication (7's)

Addition/Multiplication (8's)

Addition/Multiplication (9's)

Addition/Multiplication (10's)

Addition/Multiplication (11's)

Addition/Multiplication (12's)

Multiplication Table

Division 1

Division 2

Division 3

Division 4

Division 5

Odd Numbers

Even Numbers

Number Sentences 1

Number Sentences 2

Place Value 1/Number Sense

Place Value 2

Subtracting with Zeroes I

Subtracting with Zeroes II

Subtracting with Zeroes III

Subtracting with Zeroes IV

Subtracting with Zeroes/Review V

Fraction Practice

Names of Fractions

Writing the Names of Fractions

Writing Equivalent Fractions by Multiplying 1

Writing Equivalent Fractions by Multiplying 2

Writing Equivalent Fractions by Dividing 1

Writing Equivalent Fractions by Dividing 2

Roman Numerals

SOCIAL SCIENCE (GEOGRAPHY)

States of the United States of America

Continents

ANSWERS

Language Arts

Mathematics

Social Science (Geography)

ALL ABOUT ME will give much information about your students' abilities or lack thereof. Have them write in cursive. It will also give topics that you can use to elicit conversation and learn more about them as individuals.

ALL ABOUT ME (I AM SPECIAL!)

Name_____

First   Middle   Last

Address_____
City_____State_____ Zip code _____
Telephone number (Area code--number)_____

Birth date_____ Age_____
(Month Day Year)
School_____ Grade_____

Teacher's Name(s)_____

2 favorite subjects:
1._____ 2._____

2 favorite library books:
1._____ 2._____

2 favorite places to go:
1._____ 2._____

2 favorite TV programs:
1._____ 2._____

2 favorite foods:
1._____ 2._____

Mother's name_____
               First   Last
Father's name_____
               First   Last

How many brothers do you have? _____ Sisters?_____

I want to be a_____ when I grow up because
_____.

26 WAYS I, _____, AM WONDERFUL can be used as a homework assignment or an in-class activity. If completed at home, the students should ask their parents to assist them. That interaction can help the parents identify the many positive qualities which may have been overlooked and/or unrecognized. Parents want the very best for their children and too often forget to give praise where and when praise is due. Either way, it will help many students who, because of repeated failure, (a) don't value themselves very highly, (b) have a defeatist attitude and don't try as hard as their ability says they really can.

Name_____ Date_____

26 WAYS I, _____, AM WONDERFUL

A _____ B _____

C _____ D _____

E _____ F _____

G _____ H _____

I _____ J _____

K _____ L _____

M _____ N _____

O _____ P _____

Q _____ R _____

S _____ T _____

U _____ V _____

W _____ X _____

Y _____ Z _____

I will use all of these positive character traits, talents, and abilities to be the student every teacher would like to have, to be the friend everyone would appreciate having, and to be the child every parent would be pleased to have.

_____

Your Signature

LADDER OF SUCCESS can be used as a bulletin board, a "discussion starter" or a homework assignment. The students will identify the "rung" at which they operate most of the time, the "rung" at which they would like to operate, and what they must do to move up the ladder and become successful positive individuals.

Name_____ Date_____

LADDER OF SUCCESS
(Your ATTITUDE determines your ALTITUDE)
Where is your ATTITUDE on this ladder?

100% I DID !

90% I WILL !

80% I CAN !

70% I THINK I CAN !

60% I MIGHT TRY !

50% I SUPPOSE I SHOULD TRY !

40% WHAT IS IT?

30% I WISH I COULD.

20% I DON'T KNOW.

10% I CAN'T.

0% I WON'T.

Adaptation
Author Unknown

FOLLOWING WRITTEN DIRECTIONS can be used to help your students see the absolute importance of thinking while they read and doing what the words tell them to do. Repeat the exercises until every student completes one correctly.

AA. Read everything before you write anything.

1. Write every other capital letter of the alphabet starting with the letter

"B". _____

2. Draw 3 circles. _____

3. Draw 5 triangles. _____

4. Write your name. _____

5. Write today's date. _____

6. Draw a pentagon. _____

7. Write this numeral in words: 2,345 _____

8. Write the name of your favorite singer. _____

9. Write the number of blocks you walk to school. _____

10. Do numbers 4 and 5 ONLY. Give your paper to your teacher.

BB. Read everything before you write anything.

1. Draw 6 rectangles. _____

2. Write your name. _____

3. Write every other lower case letter of the alphabet starting with the

letter "b". _____

4. Write your mother' s name. _____

5. Write today's date. _____

6. Draw a house. _____

7. Write this numeral in words: 200,340. _____

8. Write the name of your favorite TV program._____

9. Write the number of students in your room. _____

10. Do numbers 2 and 5 and 6 ONLY. Give your paper to your teacher.

CC. Read everything before you write anything.

1. Draw 10 diamonds. _____

2. Write the odd numbers between 20 and 40. _____

3. Write the names of the 3rd, 6th, 9th, and 12th months of the year.

_____

4. Write your name. _____

5. Write today's date. _____

6. Draw a star. _____

7. Write the numerals for this number: one million._____

8. Write the name of your favorite vegetable. _____

9. Write the number of students in your room. _____

10. Do numbers 3 and 4 and 5 ONLY. Give your paper to your teacher.

DD. Read everything before you write anything.

1. Write your height. _____

2. Write five even numbers. _____

3. Write the name of your birth month. _____

4. Write the name of your favorite fruit. _____

5. Write the number of students in your room. _____

6. Draw a tree. _____

7. Write the name of this numeral in words: 1,357.

_____

8. Write your name. _____

9. Write today's date. _____

10. Do numbers 8 and 9 ONLY. Give your paper to your teacher.

EE. Read everything before you write anything.

1. Write your room number. _____

2. Write your address. _____

3. Draw one circle, two triangles, and three rectangles. _____

4. Write the number of floors in your school building. _____

5. Draw your favorite animal. _____

6. Write the name of the street your school is on. _____

7. Write your name. _____

8. Write today's date. _____

9. Complete the pattern. 9, 15, _____, _____, 33, _____.

10. Do numbers 7 and 8 ONLY. Give your paper to your teacher.

Name _____ Date _____

PARTS OF A TEXTBOOK

DIRECTIONS: Choose one of your textbooks. Give the following information.

1. What is the title of your book? The title of my book is

_____

2. What information can be found on the title page (front and back)?

A _____ B _____

C _____ D _____

E _____ F _____

3. On what page does Unit III begin? _____

3a. On what page does it end? _____

3b. Use the numbers from #3 and #3a, and figure out how many pages are in Unit III. Show your work.

_____

4. What information can be found in the Table of Contents?

A _____ B _____

C _____ D _____

5. How many chapters are in your book? _____

6. What information can you find out about a word by looking it up in the glossary? _____

_____

7. Why would you use the index? _____

_____

DICTIONARY

Choose the words for this assignment and have the students write them in the WORD BOX.

If the assigned words are chosen from a soon-to-be taught lesson, indicate the part of speech for each word as it is used in the lesson.

If the words are given in isolation (not a part of a reading assignment), indicate which part(s) of speech the students are to look for and copy those definitions or meanings only.

Name _____ Date _____

DICTIONARY

DIRECTIONS: Look up each word and record the following items: (a.) the guide words on the page where the word is found; (b.) the pronunciation; (c.) the part(s) of speech and; (d.) the meaning. Use each word in a sentence. Number the sentences and underline the word being used. Write a paragraph using all the words.

WORD BOX

_____
_____
_____
_____
_____
_____
_____
_____
_____
_____
_____
_____
_____
_____
_____
_____
_____
_____

Nettie Whitney Bailey

THESAURUS

Choose words from the daily lessons and have the students look up synonyms and antonyms.

Name _____ Date _____

THESAURUS

DIRECTIONS: Write two synonyms and two antonyms for each word. Write two sentences for each word in the Word Box, one with one of the synonyms and one with one of the antonyms. Number each sentence and underline the word being used.

WORD BOX

_____

_____
_____
_____
_____
_____
_____
_____
_____
_____
_____
_____
_____
_____
_____
_____
_____
_____
_____
_____
_____
_____

Nettie Whitney Bailey

SENTENCES, LINES, AND PARAGRAPHS

Choose a selection from the students' reader that has a limited amount of dialog. The ability to correctly answer the kinds of questions on the next page will help the students answer questions about specific parts of a selection and when discussing a selection to increase comprehension.

Name _____ Date _____

SENTENCES, LINES, AND PARAGRAPHS

DIRECTIONS: Read the assigned selection. Follow the directions and answer the questions below.

1. Copy the 4th sentence in the _____ paragraph.

_____

2. Copy the 5th line in the _____ paragraph.

_____

3. How do you recognize the beginning of a paragraph?

_____

4. How many paragraphs are there on the last page of the story_____?

5. Copy or write an interrogative sentence, one that asks a question.

_____

6. Copy or write a declarative sentence, one that states a fact and ends with a period.

_____

7. Copy or write an imperative sentence, one that tells someone or something what to do and ends with a period.

_____

8. Copy or write an exclamatory sentence, one that shows strong feeling and ends with an exclamation point.

_____

9. Write a paragraph with at least five sentences about your favorite place to go and have fun. The last sentence MUST be an exclamatory sentence, expressing your feelings about the fun you have when you go to your favorite place. Don't forget to indent the first word in your

paragraph, write capital letters where they belong, and use the correct punctuation marks.

_____

_____

_____

_____

_____

_____

_____

_____

_____

_____

_____

_____

_____

_____

_____

_____

_____

_____

_____

_____

_____

_____

_____

_____

_____

_____

DOLCH WORDS

Some of these words are found in every piece of writing. Many do not follow rules of phonics and must, therefore, be memorized. For those children who are still having trouble reading and spelling them correctly, have a spelling bee with prizes. Those students who know them can write the sentences which clarify each word's usage. Others can act as the caller or the judges.

Name _____ Date _____

DOLCH WORDS 1

DIRECTIONS: Alphabetize the words in each section, one column at a time, using 1, 2, 3, etc.

___

Section I

___know	___what	___ride	___don't	___after
___your	___carry	___with	___make	___fast
___ran	___his	___find	___of	___out
___may	___put	___stop	___came	___funny
___under	___give	___am	___but	___as

___

Section II

___has	___will	___went	___cold	___fly
___have	___here	___from	___over	___call
___some	___five	___help	___six	___it
___who	___small	___soon	___did	___buy
___if	___going	___so	___get	___that

___

Section III

___all	___ten	___run	___at	___was
___away	___my	___around	___said	___black
___this	___eat	___one	___three	___green
___little	___an	___on	___not	___yes
___her	___be	___come	___him	___brown

Name _____ Date _____

DOLCH WORDS 1a

DIRECTIONS: Alphabetize the words in each column using 1, 2, 3,etc.

I	II	III	IV	V
___know	___what	___ride	___don't	___after
___your	___carry	___with	___make	___fast
___ran	___his	___find	___of	___out
___may	___put	___stop	___came	___funny
___under	___give	___am	___but	___as
___has	___will	___went	___cold	___fly
___have	___here	___from	___over	___call
___some	___five	___help	___six	___its
___who	___small	___soon	___did	___buy
___if	___going	___so	___get	___that
___all	___ten	___run	___at	___was
___away	___my	___around	___said	___black
___this	___eat	___one	___three	___green
___little	___an	___on	___not	___yes
___her	___be	___come	___him	___brown

Name _____ Date _____

DOLCH WORDS 2

DIRECTIONS: Alphabetize the words in each section, one column at a time, using 1, 2, 3, etc.

Section I

___like	___are	___good	___can	___you
___a	___look	___no	___go	___me
___yellow	___saw	___is	___she	___had
___old	___blue	___see	___for	___up
___in	___down	___and	___he	___play

Section II

___into	___start	___its	___the	___done
___jump	___to	___use	___red	___two
___full	___big	___too	___wash	___we
___I	___ate	___hurt	___own	___shall
___because	___these	___first	___those	___do

Section III

___wish	___never	___kind	___best	___been
___try	___were	___clean	___any	___read
___better	___show	___found	___thank	___does
___far	___want	___much	___think	___bring
___always	___fall	___which	___got	___could

Name _____ Date _____

DOLCH WORDS 2a

DIRECTIONS: Alphabetize the words, one column at a time, using 1, 2, 3, etc.

I	II	III	IV	V
___like	___are	___good	___can	___you
___a	___look	___no	___go	___me
___yellow	___saw	___is	___she	___had
___old	___blue	___see	___for	___up
___in	___down	___and	___he	___play
___into	___start	___its	___the	___done
___jump	___to	___use	___red	___two
___full	___big	___too	___wash	___we
___I	___ate	___hurt	___own	___shall
___because	___these	___first	___those	___do
___wish	___never	___kind	___best	___been
___try	___were	___clean	___any	___read
___better	___show	___found	___thank	___does
___far	___want	___much	___think	___bring

___always   ___fall   ___which   ___got   ___could

Name _____ Date _____

DOLCH WORDS 3

DIRECTIONS: Alphabetize the words in each section, one column at a time, using 1, 2, 3, etc.

Section I

___gave	___draw	___goes	___pick	___off
___pull	___only	___grow	___their	___light
___four	___keep	___open	___tell	___how
___hot	___us	___well	___would	___together
___new	___hold	___once	___again	___very

Section II

___live	___right	___sing	___laugh	___seven
___ask	___warm	___made	___about	___many
___or	___just	___say	___long	___take
___they	___white	___every	___round	___today
___then	___our	___when	___write	___pretty

Section III

___upon	___let	___before	___must
___sit	___them	___where	___work
___cut	___both	___myself	___by
___these	___sleep	___drink	___why
___now	___walk	___please	___eight

Name _____ Date _____

DOLCH WORDS 3a

DIRECTIONS: Alphabetize the words one column at a time, using 1, 2, 3, etc.

I	II	III	IV	V
___gave	___draw	___goes	___pick	___off
___pull	___only	___grow	___their	___light
___four	___keep	___open	___tell	___how
___hot	___us	___well	___would	___together
___new	___hold	___once	___again	___very
___live	___right	___sing	___laugh	___seven
___ask	___warm	___made	___about	___many
___or	___just	___say	___long	___take
___they	___white	___every	___round	___today
___then	___our	___when	___write	___pretty
___upon	___let	___before	___must	___eight
___sit	___them	___where	___work	___please
___cut	___both	___myself	___by	___walk
___there	___sleep	___drink	___why	

Name _____ Date _____

INITIAL SOUNDS

DIRECTIONS: Think of the sound that each letter represents. Draw a picture or write a word that begins with each letter. Vowels can be long or short. Use your dictionary.

Aa	Bb	Cc	Dd	Ee
Ff	Gg	Hh	Ii	Jj
Kk	Ll	Mm	Nn	Oo
Pp	Qq	Rr	Ss	Tt
Uu	Vv	Ww	Xx	Yy
Zz				

Nettie Whitney Bailey

Name _____ Date _____

CAPITALIZATION & PUNCTUATION

DIRECTIONS: Rewrite the sentences, 1-10, putting capital letters and punctuation marks where they should be.

1. does your dog like to chase cats

2. her cousin keli graduated from eighth grade

3. room 213 went to the planetarium

4. what street does your uncle live on

5. watch out for that car

6. the mailman delivers the mail at 10:00 a m every morning

7. lots of people love mayor johnson

8. when my aunt jane calls me she always opens our conversations with hello how was your day

9. mr robins told his class that he saw the movie titanic ten times.

10. sarah's favorite book is mamma I wanna sing

Name _____ Date _____

CONTRACTIONS 1

When two small words are put together and one of the letters in the second word is left out and an apostrophe is put in its place, the new word is called a ***"contraction"***. Sometimes more than one letter is left out.

DIRECTIONS:

1. Read all the words in the Word Box near the bottom of this page.
2. Read each sentence. Write the 2 words that the contraction stands for. Cross out each pair of words in the Word Box as you use them.
3. Rewrite the sentence using the two words that the contraction stands for.
4. Remember -- all of these sentences begin with a capital letter and end with a period (.).

Examples:

They're going to pass to the 4th grade. They are
They are going to pass to the 4th grade.

Hurry, or we'll miss the bus. we will
Hurry, or we will miss the bus.

WORD BOX

would not	he is	Can not	we are	I am

1. He's going to Disney World for his birthday. _____

1a. _____

2. My mother can't drive a car with a stick shift. _____

2a. _____

3. We're going to read two books every week. _____

3a. _____

4. I'm going to be late for school. _____

4a. _____

5. My father wouldn't let us watch WWF last night. _____

5a. _____

DIRECTIONS: Write the contractions for the words below. Use each one in a sentence.

6. could not   _____

7. I will   _____
_____

8. she is   _____
_____

9. we have   _____
_____

10. they are   _____
_____

Name _____ Date _____

CONTRACTIONS 2

When two small words are put together and one of the letters in the second word is left out and an apostrophe is put in its place, the new word is called a ***"contraction"***. Sometimes more than one letter is left out.

DIRECTIONS:

1. Read all the words in the Word Box.
2. Read each sentence.
3. Write the 2 words that the contraction stands for and cross out each pair in the Word Box as you use it.
4. Rewrite the sentence using the two words that the contraction stands for.
5. Notice -- all of these sentences begin with a capital letter and end with a period (.).

Examples:

She's going to pass to 6th grade. She is
She is going to pass to the 6th grade.

Hurry, or we'll miss the bus. we will
Hurry, or we will miss the bus.

WORD BOX

would not	were not	should not	could not	I am
will not	have not	She will	can not	He is
They are	did not	I have	We are	I will

63

1. He's going to the store. _____
1a. _____
2. My two-year old brother can't tie his shoes. _____
2a. _____
3. We're going to finish all of our homework. _____
3a. _____
4. I'm going to be late for school. _____
4a. _____
5. Sam wouldn't eat because he does not like oatmeal. _____
5a. _____
6. I am out of breath because I've been running. _____
6a. _____
7. She'll bite you if you bother her puppies. _____
7a. _____
8. The baby won't eat because he is sick. _____
8a. _____
9. My grandmother couldn't find her umbrella._____
9a. _____
10. They're going to Pete's birthday party. _____
10a. _____
11. She got in trouble because she didn't wash the dishes._____
11a. _____
12. I'll watch Barney with my little sister tomorrow morning._____
12a. _____
13. There weren't any cars parked on the street. _____
13a. _____
14. You shouldn't do your math problems with a pen._____
14a. _____
15. I haven't been to the show to see Mulan yet. _____
15a. _____

Name _____ Date _____

NOUN MARKERS (ARTICLES)

A *noun marker* (article) is a word that introduces/precedes a noun. A *noun* is a word that names a person, a place, or a thing. A **verb** is a word that shows action. It tells you what someone is doing, what someone did, or what someone is going to do.

DIRECTIONS: Complete the chart. Write eleven nouns and eleven verbs.

Noun Markers		Nouns	Verbs
1.	The	boy	ran
2.	A		
3.	An		
4.	Those		
5.	That		
6.	My		
7.	His		
8.	Your		
9.	Her		
10.	Their		
11.	The		
12.	Our		

Name _____

DIRECTIONS: Write complete sentences using each noun marker, noun, and verb from the chart. Add other words to make the sentences interesting and exciting. Underline the words from the chart.
Example: <u>The</u> short <u>boy</u> <u>ran</u> and jumped and dunked the basketball.

1. _____
2. _____
3. _____
4. _____
5. _____
6. _____
7. _____
8. _____
9. _____
10. _____
11. _____
12. _____

CHALLENGE.

Choose a subject. Choose twelve (12) nouns and twelve (12) verbs related to your subject and write them on the back of your paper. Write a paragraph using those words. Remember . . .

1. indent the first word of the paragraph.
2. to have a beginning, a middle, and an end.

_____
_____
_____
_____
_____
_____
_____

Name _____ Date _____

NOUNS

A noun is a word that tells you the name of a person (someone you know), a place (where you can go), or a thing (something you can show).

Examples: Common nouns -- boy, school, toy
Proper nouns -- Arthur, Yale, Play Station

DIRECTIONS: Write three common or proper nouns for each letter.

	Person/People	Places	Things
Aa	Albert	airport	aardvark
Bb	barber	bowling alley	balloon
Cc			
Dd			
Ee			
Ff			
Gg			
Hh			
Ii			
Jj			
Kk			
Ll			
Mm			
Nn			
Oo			

	Person/People	Places	Things
Pp			
Qq			
Rr			
Ss			
Tt			
Uu			
Vv			
Ww			
Xx	Xavier	Xerox Company	xylophone
Yy			
Zz			

Name _____

DIRECTIONS: Choose five letters and circle them. Write one sentence using each type of noun that begins with the letters you chose.

Examples: 1. Xavier lives on the second floor.
2. The <u>Xerox Company</u> is located on Illinois Avenue.
3. Would you like to learn how to play the xylophone?

1. _____

2. _____

3. _____

1. _____

2. _____

3. _____

1. _____

2. _____

3. _____

1. _____

2. _____

3. _____

1. _____

2. _____

3. _____

Name _____ Date _____

COMMON AND PROPER NOUNS, VERBS AND ADJECTIVES

DIRECTIONS: Write ten common nouns, ten proper nouns, ten verbs, and ten adjectives. Remember, proper nouns begin with capital letters.

Common Nouns	Proper Nouns	Verbs	Adjectives

DIRECTIONS: Write ten sentences. Use all four words in each sentence. Number your sentences and underline the words from the chart.

Examples: The little boy saw Mr. Brown
(A,   CN,   V,   PN)

Waiting for the bus makes old Mrs. Waters tired.
   V,   CN,   A,   PN)

Waiting for the bus makes old Mrs. Waters tired.
   V,   CN,   A,   PN)

Children enjoy eating at busy McDonald's.
(CN   V,   A,   PN)

71

Name _____

1 _____

_____

2 _____

_____

3 _____

_____

4 _____

_____

5 _____

_____

6 _____

_____

7 _____

_____

8 _____

   _____

9 _____

   _____

10 _____

   _____

Name _____ Date _____

NOUNS, VERBS & ADJECTIVES 1

Common nouns are words that tell you the name of any person, any place, or any thing. Proper nouns name specific persons, places, or things.

Examples: Common nouns -- boy, city, toys
Proper nouns -- Mike, Chicago, Play Station

Verbs are words that show action or a state of being. They can tell you what someone is doing, what someone did, or what someone is going to do. They can also tell what someone or something is or was.

Examples: reading, playing, thinking, read, played, thought
will read, will play, will think
("will" is called a helping verb.)

Adjectives are words that describe. They tell you how a noun looks, smells, sounds, tastes, or feels.

Examples: shiny, good, loud, delicious, smooth, expensive

DIRECTIONS: Complete the chart by writing a noun, a verb, and an adjective that begin with each letter.

Name _____

	Nouns	Verbs	Adjectives
Aa			
Bb			
Cc			
Dd			
Ee			

	Nouns	Verbs	Adjectives
Ff			
Gg			
Hh			
Ii			
Jj			

	Nouns	Verbs	Adjectives
Kk			
Ll			
Mm			
Nn			
Oo			

Nettie Whitney Bailey

Name _____

	Nouns	Verbs	Adjectives
Pp			
Qq			
Rr			
Ss			
Tt			

	Nouns	Verbs	Adjectives
Uu			
Vv			
Ww			
Xx			
Yy			
Zz			

DIRECTIONS: Choose two groups of letters (A-E, F-J, K-O, P-T, or U-Z). Write one sentence using the noun, the verb, and the adjective that begin with each of the letters in that group. If necessary, use other words to make the sentences funnier or more interesting. Number your sentences and underline the words you used from the chart.

Example: Carol cut cucumbers.
Helen has a hundred hairy hamsters.

Name _____ Date _____

NOUNS, VERBS, AND ADJECTIVES 2

DIRECTIONS: Fill in the blanks.

A noun is a word that names a _____, a _____, or a
_____. It names somebody or something that you can look at, go to,
or touch.
Verbs are words that show . _____ or _____.
An adjective is a word that _____. It tells what kind or how
something _____, how something _____, how
something _____, how something _____, or how
something _____. Adjectives involve the 5 senses.

DIRECTIONS: Read the words in the Word Box. Read the sentences
and underline ALL the nouns. Fill the blanks with words from the Word
Box. Cross out each word as you use it. Identify the kind of word you
wrote in the blank by writing N, or V, or Adj. in the blank at the end of
each sentence.

Study this example:

<u>People</u> all over the <u>world</u> like to <u>watch</u> <u>Michael Jordan</u> play <u>basketball</u>.

Read these questions and think about the answers:

Why is "People" underlined?
<u>People is underlined because it names people.</u>

Why is "world" underlined?
<u>World is underlined because it names a place.</u>

Why is "Michael Jordan" underlined?
<u>Michael Jordan is underlined because it names a specific person.</u>

Nettie Whitney Bailey

Name _____

Why is "basketball" underlined?
Basketball is underlined because it names a thing, a sport.

Why is the verb "watch" written in the blank instead of the noun watch?
The verb watch is written because that is what the people are doing.

Read the DIRECTIONS again. Complete your assignment.

WORD BOX

shade, n.	shade, n.	paint, n.	paint,	v. train,	n. train, v.
park, n.	park, v.	fine, n.	fine, adj.	pipe, n.	pipe, v.
box, n.	box, v.	watch, n.	watch, v.	type, n.	type, v.
wave, n.	wave, v.	back, n.	back, adj.	swing, n.	swing, v.

1. Mr. Green said we can get extra credit if we _____ our book reports. _____
2. My boss said that I did a _____ job. _____
3. Pull the _____ down so that the sun won't fade the couch cover. _____
4. Mama said, "Be careful! _____ what you are doing so that you don't knock my plant over. _____
5. I wish I could have seen Muhammad Ali _____ in person. _____
6. It took many hours to _____ the elephants. _____
7. Susan and her brother took Judy to the _____ to _____. _____ _____

78

8 . I taught my baby sister to _____ bye-bye. _____

9. Mrs. Williams wants Tony to _____ her _____ porch. _____ _____

10. When you take your driving test, you will have to _____ the car. _____

11. The _____ of vehicle you will drive determines the kind of license you will need. _____

12. Drivers who exceed the speed limit will get a ticket and pay a_____._____

13. Mr. Jordan's sun glasses _____ his eyes from the sun. _____

14. Mrs. Hernandez bought a gallon of expensive _____ for her daughter's backyard _____. _____ _____

15. We are going to take the _____ when we visit our grandmother. _____

16. I like to smell the tobacco my uncle smokes in his _____ . _____

17. Jesse received a waterproof _____ for graduation because he likes to swim. _____

18. Experienced surfers compete to see who can ride the biggest _____. _____

19. One of the New York Knicks hurt his _____ in a playoff game. _____

20. They moved so far away from the city, they had to either dig a well or _____ their water into their new home.

Name _____

Challenge:

DIRECTIONS: List all the pronouns in the sentences. There are almost 40! Write the number you identified in the blank.

_____

_____

_____

_____

_____

I _____ identified _____ pronouns.

NOUNS, PRONOUNS, VERBS, AND ADJECTIVES

This can be started as a class activity and completed as a small group or individual activity. Have the students read the sentences and identify the nouns, pronouns, verbs, and adjectives. Remind them that many words have multiple meanings and can represent more than one part of speech. Have them identify the noun that each pronoun takes the place of.

Name _____ Date _____

NOUNS, PRONOUNS, VERBS, AND ADJECTIVES

Remember -- nouns name people, places, and things.

      -- pronouns take the place of nouns; refer to nouns.

      -- adjectives precede (come right before) nouns and describe nouns.

      -- verbs tell what someone/something is doing or what someone/something is or was.

      -- some words can be used as more than one part of speech

DIRECTIONS: Read the sentences.

1. Mr. Green said we can get extra credit if we type our book reports.

2. After he read Tony's report, he said he had done a fine job.

3. Pull the shade down so that the sun won't fade the couch cover.

4. Mama said, "Be careful, watch what you're doing so that you don't knock my plant over when you pull it down.

5. I wish I could have seen Muhammad Ali box in person.

6. He had to train many, many hours.

7. Susan and her brother took Judy to the park to swing.

8. Susan taught her baby sister, Judy, to wave bye-bye.

9. Mrs. Williams wants Tony to paint her back porch.

10. She promised to pay him thirty dollars if he does a good job.

11. When you take your driving test, you will have to park the car.

12. The type vehicle you will drive determines the kind of license you will need.

13. The suit Mr. Jordan bought is a very nice shade of brown.

14. He plans to paint his porch swing the same color.

15. We are going to take the train when we visit our grandparents.

16. I like to smell the tobacco my grandfather smokes in his pipe.

17. Jesse received a waterproof watch for graduation because he likes to go surfing.

18. He hopes to become an experienced surfer and ride a huge wave.

19. The Reynolds family grew tired of the noise and fast pace of the big city.

20. They moved to a rural area and were able to see a star-studded sky because there was no pollution to hide them from view.

DIRECTIONS: Reread sentences 1 and 2. Notice where each word has been placed in the chart and why. "If" is not on the chart because it is a different part of speech. Choose ten sentences (five pair). Circle their numbers. Complete. the chart by writing the words from the sentences you chose in the proper columns.

Name _____

Adjective	Noun	Verb	Pronoun
1. extra	Mr. Green, credit, report	said, can, get, type	we, we, our
2. good	Tony's, report, job	read, said, had done	he, he, he

Name _____ Date _____

MULTIPLE MEANINGS

DIRECTIONS: Look up the words in the Word Box in your dictionary. Write the number of meanings for each word. Write one definition for the noun (n.), one for the verb (v.), and one for the adjective (adj.). Write one sentence for each. Study this example.

<u>8</u> back, n. -- the rear part of an object serving to support or protect.
My brothers were playing and broke the back of the kitchen chair.
<u>8</u> back, v. -- endorse
Be sure and back your check before you put it in the bank.
<u>5</u> back, adj. -- belong to the past
My teacher told us to go to the library and read a back issue of Ebony magazine.

WORD BOX				
bar	scratch	fire	pit	address

1. bar
___ n. _____
___ v. _____
___ adj. _____

2. scratch
___ n. _____
___ v. _____
___ adj. _____

3. fire

___ n. _____

___ v. _____

___ adj. _____

4. pit

___ n. _____

___ v. _____

___ adj. _____

5. address

___ n. _____

___ v. _____

___ adj. _____

Challenge.

DIRECTION: Using the words above, write five sentences using all three parts of speech in each sentence.

Example: Daddy wouldn't lean against the ***back*** of his chair when he ***backed*** his paycheck or even when he read ***back*** issues of People magazine.

1. _____

2. _____

3. _____

4. _____

5. _____

SINGULAR, PLURAL & POSSESSIVE NOUNS
PRONOUN CONTRACTIONS

DIRECTIONS: Fill in the blanks with the words from the chart.

Singular nouns (one)	Plural nouns (more than one)	Pronoun contractions (Apostrophe takes the place of a letter(s)	Possessive nouns (Something belongs)
Julie	girls	she's---they'll	Julie's--girls'
George	boys	he's---they'll	George's--boys'

1. Five _____ in my room are cheerleaders.

_____

2. _____ cheer at the basketball game.

_____

3. The _____ skirts are green and white.

_____

4. _____ will miss the game because she goes to another school.

_____

5. I hope _____ new teacher helps her learn to read better.

_____

6. The _____ on the team can run fast.

7. The _____ t-shirts are white.

8. If they practice hard, _____ win lots of games.

9. Is _____ on the team?

10. Yes, _____ the best scorer on the team.

11. Ms. Foster put all of _____ papers in a green folder.

12. _____ looking at her records to find out who'll get special gifts.

Name _____ Date _____

DIRECTIONS. Write four sentences, one with each of the following: a singular noun, a plural noun, a contraction, and a possessive noun. Do not use any of the words on the chart.

1 _____

2. _____

3.. _____

4. _____

EIGHT PARTS OF SPEECH

This assignment is designed for older students who are still not sure about parts of speech. It can be a class activity with the class divided into maybe 6 groups -- 1. nouns 2. verbs 3. adjectives 4. adverbs 5. pronouns and 6. conjunctions, prepositions, interjections, and noun markers. Only your creativity limits its use.

Suggested follow-up exercises.

1. Have one student choose a noun marker and write it on the chalk-board, the first word in a sentence that several students will complete. Direct other students to choose and write an adjective, a noun, a verb, an adverb, a preposition, another noun marker, and a noun. Discuss subject (What is the sentence about?) and predicate (What did the subject do?)
   Example: The big dog ran quickly up the stairs.

2. Have the students to write sentences with an assigned number of words.
   Example: Three words. The baby cried.

2a. Add 2 adjectives and an adverb.
    Example: The cute, little baby cried loudly.

2b. Make the sentence more interesting by telling why she cried.
    Example: The cute, little baby cried loudly when she dropped her bottle.

2c. Make the sentence more interesting by telling what happened to the bottle when it hit the floor.
    Example: The cute, little baby cried loudly when she dropped her bottle and it rolled under the bed.

Name _____ Date _____

EIGHT PARTS OF SPEECH

Read ALL directions before you write ANYTHING.

DIRECTIONS. Use the glossary in your English book or the dictionary. Write your answers in complete sentences. See Example in #1. Be sure capital letters are where they belong!

1. What is a noun?   A noun is a word that names a person, a place, or a thing. _____

   Proper nouns name _____

2. What is a pronoun? A pronoun is _____

3. What is a verb? _____

   Give an example. _____

4. What is an adjective? _____

   Give an example. _____

5. What is an adverb? _____

   Give an example. _____

6. What is a conjunction? _____

   Give an example. _____

7. What is a preposition? _____

   Give an example. _____

8. What is an interjection? _____

   Give an example. _____

9. What is a noun marker (article)? _____
   Give an example.

   _____

   _____

Name _____   Date _____

EIGHT PARTS OF SPEECH

DIRECTIONS. Write a word for each part of speech using each letter of the alphabet. Use the dictionary to complete the chart if there are empty boxes that you cannot fill.

	Noun	Pronoun	Verb	Adjective	Adverb	Conjunction	Preposition	Interjection
Aa								
Bb								
Cc								
Dd								
Ee								
Ff								
Gg								
Hh								
Ii								
Jj								
Kk								

Nettie Whitney Bailey

Name _____

Date _____

	Noun	Pronoun	Verb	Adjective	Adverb	Conjunction	Preposition	Interjection
Ll								
Mm								
Nn								
Oo								
Pp								
Qq								
Rr								
Ss								
Tt								
Uu								
Vv								
Ww								
Xx								
Yy								
Zz								

Name _____ Date _____

PRONOUNS AND ANTECEDENTS

DIRECTIONS: Write five nouns in the spaces under "Nouns" and a pronoun in each space under "Pronouns" that can take its place.

Nouns	Pronouns
Example: teacher	*Example*: she
1.	
2.	
3.	
4.	
5.	

DIRECTIONS: Write a sentence using each noun. Then write a second related sentence using the pronoun.

Example: My teacher gives us lots of homework.
            She has to mark all of our papers..

1. _____
1. _____

2. _____
2. _____

3. _____
3. _____

4. _____
4. _____

5. _____

5. _____

DIRECTED READING LESSON
(Realistic Fiction)
(Written activity gives practice identifying pronoun antecedents)

VOCABULARY

Present words that you think the students may be able to pronounce but not know the meaning of, remembering that many words have multiple meanings. Discuss such words.

Example: Douglas, n. -- a boy's first name; a surname/family name
Douglas, adj. -- paragraph 1 -- a kind of fir tree

_____

_____

_____

ROOT WORDS/AFFIXES

Present words that have affixes. Discuss their root words and how each affix changes the meaning.

earthquake(s)	erupt(ed)	
neighbor(ing)	sand(y)	
eventual(ly)	special(ist)	
need(less)	(un)told	(micro)scope

CAPITALIZATION/PUNCTUATION

Identify all the words that begin with capital letters and tell why they begin with capitals.

COMPREHENSION

Review and follow suggestions on page 10. Write the questions you will use to check for understanding during the discussion. Help the students understand the difference between realistic fiction (something that could really happen but didn't) and make-believe.

Factual/Literal

1. _____
1. _____
1. _____

Interpretive

2. _____
2. _____
2. _____

Evaluative

3. _____
3. _____
3. _____

EXTENDED LEARNING

Have the students look up information on other volcanos, finding out where they are located and what happened when they erupted.

FUN

Have the students, using the letters in **pneu-mo-no-ul-tra-mi-cro-sco-pic-si-li-co-vol-ca-no-con-i-o-sis,** make new words. Assign point value to the words: 2-letter words, 2 points; 3-letter words, 3 points; 4-letter words, 4 points, etc.

Name _____ Date _____

DIRECTIONS: Read the story. Write an ending. Give the story a title.

_____

In March of 1980, there were several earthquakes in the state of Washington. As a result, on May 18 of that same year, the volcano in Mount Saint Helens erupted after sleeping for one hundred twenty-three years. (1) It sent dust and debris twelve miles into the sky. (2) They filled lakes and rivers A forest of Douglas fir trees was destroyed. Untold numbers of animals, fish, and birds were killed. More than a score of humans lost (3) their lives and many more were injured.

Rescue workers came from the east, south, mid-west, and from neighboring states to help. (4) They worked long hours for several weeks. Years later, internists at four hospitals in four different states were baffled. (5) They each had patients who were exhibiting the same strange symptoms. After running many, many tests and conferring with each other and with lung specialists across the country, (6) they found that all the patients had assisted in the rescue efforts after Mount St. Helens woke up. Each one had worked for a brief period of time without a gas mask. (7) They inhaled a lot of the volcanic dust (8) that eventually made (9) them sick. Those doctors were, needless to say, very happy and quite relieved once (10) they found out what had made (11) their patients sick. (12) That made it possible for (13) them to devise a treatment plan and, hopefully, help the patients regain their health and strength.

(14) Their disease didn't have a name. The doctors who worked so hard to help the patients called (15) it pneu-mo-no-ul-tra-mi-cro-sco-pic-si-li-co-vol-ca-no-con-i-o-sis because the lungs were affected and the sandy dust particles that came from the volcano were so small that (16) they could only be seen under a high-powered microscope.

_____

_____

_____

_____

Name _____

DIRECTIONS: Write the noun that each of the numbered pronouns stands for.

1 _____ 2 _____ 3 _____
4 _____ 5 _____ 6 _____
7 _____ 8 _____ 9 _____
10 _____ 11 _____ 12 _____
13 _____ 14 _____ 15 _____
16 _____

Name _____ Date _____

HOMONYMS 1

DIRECTIONS: Read the homonyms in the word box. Use each one in a sentence. Number each sentence and underline the homonym. Do not guess. Use your dictionary to check the meanings.

WORD BOX

do   dew   flower   flour   sun   son   some   sum   would   wood
won   one   too   two   to

Name _____ Date _____

HOMONYMS 2

DIRECTIONS: Read the homonyms in the word box. Write a story using all of the homonyms. Underline them. Use your dictionary to check the meanings you are not sure of.

WORD BOX

hour   our   ten   tin   eight   ate   right   write   one   won   knot   not
  close   clothes   they're   their   there

_____

_____

_____

_____

_____

_____

_____

_____

_____

_____

_____

_____

_____

_____

_____

_____

_____

SUBJECTS FOR CREATIVE WRITING
(Narrative, Descriptive or Expository)

These subjects can be used as individual assignments or as small group activities. Individuals can be given the opportunity to choose their topic; the small group topics should be assigned.

Time-saving tip.

When giving an assignment, have the students concentrate on only one or two of the following:

1. complete sentences
2. correct capitalization
3. correct punctuation
4. correct spelling
5. ideas
6. organization (beginning, middle, end)

This will make marking their work much easier.

If you . . .

. . . found a bag containing ten $500 bills and no identifying information, what would you do? Why? (Have the students figure out how much that is.)

. . . were blind or deaf, what could you do to make life worth living?

If you could . . .

. . . learn to play any instrument, which one would you choose? Why? Who would you want to be your teacher?

. . . have an extra father, who would you choose? Why? What would you want him to do?

. . . live anywhere in the world, where would you live? Why?

. . . invent anything, what would it be? Who would it help? How would it help them?

. . . go to any high school, which one would it be? Why? What subjects would you enjoy the most? Which ones would you not want to take? Why? In what extra-curricular activities would you participate?

. . . own a business what kind would it be? Why? Who would you have working for you? If it's a store, what would you sell? If it's a restaurant, what kind would it be? Why? What would your specialty be if you offered a variety of foods? Who would do the cooking? How would you choose your waiters and waitresses? Why would people come to your business and not another one just like yours?

. . . be in a fairy tale, which one would you choose? Why? Who or what would you be? Would you do anything differently than the original character?

If you could be . . .

. . . invisible, name 3 things you would do. Why? Where would you go? Why?

. . . mayor of a city, which city would it be? Why? Name at least three things you would do and tell why you believe they are necessary.

. . . principal of your school, name at least three changes you would make and why.

. . . teacher in your classroom, name three changes you would make and why.

. . . manager of your school's lunchroom, name three changes you would make and why. Create lunch menus for one week.

If you could be a . . .

. . . farm animal, which one would you be? Why?

. . . singer, what kind(s) of songs would you sing? Why?

. . . doctor, what kind would you be? Why?

. . . professional athlete, what sport would you choose? Why? If it's a team sport, which team would you want to be a part of?

. . . policeman, how would you want to help the people?

SUBJECTS FOR CREATIVE WRITING
(Persuasion)

Write six (6) of the items shown below on the chalkboard. Have the students choose one of the categories and think about their favorite thing in that category. On a piece of scratch paper, have them write words they think they might use. If there are words whose spelling they are not sure of, have them raise their hands, say them, and you write them on the chalkboard. Then, have them write a paragraph to convince a friend why their favorite should be their friend's favorite too.

TV show	color	vegetable	city to visit
way to travel	make and color of car		fruit
spectator sport	TV personality		invention

READ-ALOUD STORY

Students are never too old to be read to. As they listen, they become more familiar with the flow of language, language usage, and how the voice changes as a result of certain punctuation marks.

Stop, if necessary, to be sure the students understand unfamiliar vocabulary. Ask a few questions during or after the story to check for understanding. Discuss the story --

What they liked.

What they disliked.

What they already know about the subject.

What they learned about the subject.

What they would like to learn about the subject.

Have the students retell the story.

OMAR
by
Nettie Whitney Bailey

I really don't want to be in the circus. When I told Mother how I felt, she said, "Your father and I have been with this same circus for twenty years. We have never wanted for anything. We've been **all** over this country, traveling in the best wagons in the whole circus. We've been the stars of the Big Top because Glenn has always created unique tricks for us to do and he's **never** been mean to us. Why-y-y would you want to leave?" Huge tears filled her big beautiful eyes, ran down sagging cheeks and created two dark circles in the thin layer of straw which covered the floor of our tent.

I was sorry I had said anything, but I had to be honest. "Mother, I always do the very best I can when Glenn has us practicing or we're learning a new trick, even though my heart isn't in it." I started to cry, partly because my words had made Mother sad and partly because I was so frustrated. I just don't enjoy what I'm doing. Even when it's opening night in a new town and everybody is excited, I'm sad. Sometimes I smile a little. One day, I even laughed when a teeny, tiny, black car rattled into the arena from behind the shimmering entrance curtain. It looked like it was too small even for the two clowns whose red, tennis ball noses I could see through the windshield. It made a couple of jerky trips around the first ring, belching giant puffs of pink smoke. *Six* clowns, short, tall, fat, and skinny, soon came tumbling out doing cartwheels and playing leapfrog all around that ring. Bright red, wide, floppy shoes, shiny, narrow, black shoes, long, spiked multicolored hair, and tall, tall top hats, flew in every direction. It really felt good to laugh, but that good feeling just didn't last. I didn't want to be there.

One bright spring day, Glenn sat just outside our tent resting and watching television. That wasn't unusual. What *was* unusual, was that he wasn't asleep five minutes after he sat down! When I didn't hear him snoring, I pushed the flap aside and stuck my head out so that I could see what was keeping him awake. It was a show all about elephants. I watched. I haven't been the same since. I saw large families. . . little babies, boys and girls my size, mothers, fathers, aunts and uncles, and some members that looked like they might have been grandparents! I saw them swimming! I saw them flinging dust. I didn't know why they were doing that, but it looked like fun. I really laughed when I saw one great big bull rubbing his backside up and down on the rough bark of a tree. That really must have felt good.

My excitement turned to fear when the narrator described how poachers hunted and killed elephants to get their ivory. I wished I had never seen that part. As horrible as it was, it didn't change my mind. I still wanted to leave. Before I could make plans to leave, something happened.

We learned a new trick for the opening matinee in Chicago. After the ring master, in his bright red coat, black riding pants, black patent leather knee-high boots and top hat, greeted the customers, he said there was a special "Welcome!" he had to give. The winners of the Special Olympics were our extraordinary guests. He explained that all the children were winners; not just those who won the games and received medals, but every child that played was a winner, because they made the best of their limitations . . . blindness, mental retardation, missing limbs, limbs that don't work . . . and they lived happy, busy lives.

We were anxious. Glenn worked to keep us calm while we waited for our turn. We are always the last act before the finale, the grand parade. Finally, we heard the ringmaster. "And now, the act you've been waiting for, the smartest Indian elephants in the whole wide world! And here they are!" The conductor raised his baton and the band filled the air with our song, "Here Come The Elephants." The entrance curtain was drawn to the right. We trotted into the arena flapping our ears, our toe nails polished with neon colors and wearing our new tasseled outfits. We were met with thunderous applause. Glenn rode in on Father's back. He sat proudly in an elegant howdah, filled with big silk pillows . . . turquoise, gold, and magenta. His print shirt matched the pillows and the intricate design that Griff, one of the clowns, had painted on the howdah. That fancy box was a first for us. Glenn usually rode into the center ring on a brightly colored, but plain, wooden chair perched precariously on Father's wide back.

We completed our regular routine; each one of us standing, with all four feet on stools that looked too small to hold either one of us. We rolled big beach balls around the ring and tossed them to Glenn. We posed with our feet on the back of the elephant in front of us, except for Tina, the baby. She held onto seven-year-old Champ's tail with her trunk.

Griff and the other clowns, Sandy, Red, Felix, Angie, and Phil, struggled into the arena, knees buckling as they carried what appeared to be a very heavy barrel. They set it down with a thud just inside the center ring. They tugged and tugged to pull out whatever was in that barrel. They all yelled "Gotcha!" as they each yanked out a limp balloon and held it up.

We inflated the balloons using the special pumps which Glenn had designed. He and the clowns removed them from the helium tanks when they were full and tied them on sticks that had a toy elephant at the other end. Mother, Father and the other old ones placed the great big balloons, which were on five-foot sticks, in holders anchored to the center ring. They were then led over to the far side of the arena holding basketball-sized balloons on shorter sticks. Waiting for them were the ten children whose ticket stubs had a gold star. Each one of them received a balloon

. . . from one of the old ones! When the four younger ones and I got our balloons, we were led over to the section where our special guests were sitting. There were five children in wheelchairs waiting for us. We gave them our balloons. Their big smiles and their giggles gave me a feeling I *could not* explain. I, Omar, an ordinary twelve-year-old, caused a child to smile. I now understood why Mother and Father have been so willing to remain with the circus. It's the giving . . . making others happy . . . especially children.

That feeling, an indescribably good feeling, didn't go away, so I decided to stay.

MATH LANGUAGE

This can be used to assess some of the needs of the students It can also be used to provide review as well as fun. As a fun-type activity, it is suggested that it be used only after you have determined whether or not the majority of students can experience a satisfactory level of success.

Inform or remind the students that for many, many years, lots of people believed that boys were smarter than girls in subjects like math and science.

"Let's see who remembers the most math language, boys or girls." Direct the boys to stand on one side of the room and the girls on the other. Give each group a couple of minutes to choose a recorder, students who will write down the correct answers. Give the directions or ask the questions. The students who give the correct responses score a point for their team. Have the recorders exchange papers. Read the answers, determine the "Winner for the Day" -- the team that gave the most correct answers. Encourage the "losers" by explaining the importance of hard work which will help them reach their goal . . . to become what they want to be as recorded on their "ALL ABOUT ME" assignment.

1. Name the answer to an addition problem. (Sum)

2. Name the answer to a subtraction problem. (Difference)

3. Name the answer to a multiplication problem. (Product, Multiple)

4. Name the answer to a division problem. (Quotient)

5. Name the numerals in an addition problem. (Addends)

6. Name the top numeral in a subtraction problem. (Minuend)

7. Name the bottom numeral in a subtraction problem. (Subtrahend)

8. Name the numerals in a multiplication problem. (Factors)

9. Name the bottom numeral in a multiplication problem. (Multiplier)

10. Name the numeral to the right of the division sign or outside the box in a division problem. (Divisor)

11. Name the number to the left of the division sign or inside the box in a division problem. (Dividend)

12. Write/name the symbol/sign that tells you to add. (+ Plus sign)

13. Write/name the symbol/sign that tells you to subtract. (Minus sign)

14. Write/name the symbol/sign that tells you that two numerals or number sentences are the same. (= Equal sign)

15. Write/name the symbol/sign that tells you to multiply. (× Multiplication sign)

16. Write one of the symbols/signs that tells you to divide. (or ÷)

17. Write the symbol/sign for greater than. (>)

18. Write the symbol/sign for less than. (<)

19. Write the fraction one-tenth (1/10)

20. Write the fraction three-one hundredth (3/100)

21. Write the fraction five-one thousandth (5/1000)

22. Write the numerator in #19. (1)

23. Write the denominator in #21. (1,000)

24. Write a proper fraction using the numerals 3 and 4. (3/4)

25. Write an improper fraction using the numerals 5 and 6. (6/5)

26. Write a mixed number. (Any combination of a whole number and a fraction is acceptable, such as 5 ½ .)

27. When writing decimals, tenth means there will be _____ numeral following the decimal point. (one,.4)

28. When writing decimals, hundredth means there will be _____ numerals following the decimal point. (two, .03 or .56)

29. When writing decimals, thousandths means there will be _____ numerals following the decimal point. (three, .007 or .085 or .379)

30. Write one-tenth as a decimal. (.1)

31. Write three-hundredths as a decimal. (.03)

32. Write five-thousandths as a decimal. (.005)

33. Write this numeral on the chalkboard, two hundred forty-five thousand nine hundred sixty-seven. (245, 967)

34. What is the value of the 2? (200,000)

35. Describe/draw a circle. (Flat figure that looks like a ball)

36. Name the term that describes all four-sided figures. (Quadrilateral)

37. Describe/draw a square. (Four-sided figure, all sides equal)

38. Describe/draw a rectangle. (Four-sided figure, 2 equal widths, 2 equal lengths)

39. Describe/draw a triangle (Three-sided figure)

40. Describe/draw a pentagon. (Five-sided figure, all sides equal)

41. Describe/draw a hexagon. (Six-sided figure, all sides equal)

42. Describe/draw an octagon. (Eight-sided figure, all sides equal)

43. Describe/draw a cube. (Solid six-sided figure, all sides equal)

44. Describe/draw a cone. (Solid figure that looks like an ice cream cone.)

45. Describe/draw a cylinder (Solid figure that looks like a soup can)

Nettie Whitney Bailey

Name _____ Date _____

ADDITION FACTS 1

DIRECTIONS: Add from top to bottom. Check your answers by adding from bottom to top.

1. 2 6 8 5 6 7 4 5 4 3 8 7 3
    9 7 5 6 4 8 5 5 9 8 5 6 9

2. 3 7 8 3 4 5 4 7 6 5 8 6 2
    9 6 5 8 9 5 8 4 6 5 4 7 9

3. 2 6 9 4 2 7 2 5 5 9 3 2 9
    9 7 1 8 8 6 8 8 6 4 9 9 3

4. 2 6 8 5 6 7 4 5 4 3 8 7 3
    9 7 4 5 6 4 8 5 9 8 5 6 9

5. 3 7 8 3 4 5 4 7 6 5 8 6 2
    9 6 5 8 9 5 8 4 6 5 4 7 9

6. 2 6 9 4 2 7 2 5 5 9 3 2 9
    9 7 1 8 8 6 8 8 6 4 9 9 3

114

1A. DIRECTIONS: Fill in the blanks. **Hint.** To find the missing numeral, subtract the smaller numeral from the larger numeral.

Example: 3 + ___ = 10 Solution: 10 - 3 = 7 So: 3 + 7 = 10

1.	12 + ___ = 12	7 + ___ = 12	___ + 9 = 12	4 + ___ = 12
2.	10 + ___ = 12	___ + 8 = 12	6 + ___ = 12	___ + 11 = 12
3.	___ + 10 = 13	___ + 8 = 13	___ + 7 = 13	___ + 9 = 13
4.	5 + ___ = 13	___ + 1 = 13	___ + 2 = 13	___ + 4 = 13
5.	4 + ___ = 10	5 + ___ = 10	___ =+ 1 = 10	___ + 2 = 10
6.	10 + ___ = 10	7 + ___ = 10	3 + ___ = 10	1 + ___ = 10
7.	5 + ___ = 11	___ + 1 = 11	___ + 2 = 11	3 + ___ = 13
8.	___ + 1 = 11	___ + 4 = 11	___ + 9 = 11	___ + 11 = 11
9.	1 + ___ = 12	3 + ___ = 12	5 + ___ = 12	___ + 9 = 12
10.	___ + 1 = 12	___ + 2 = 12	9 + ___ = 12	1 + ___ = 12
11.	11 + ___ = 13	___ + 2 = 13	___ + 6 = 13	13 + ___ = 13
12.	___ + 0 = 10	0 + ___ = 13	0 + ___ = 11	___ + 10 = 10
13.	12 + ___ = 13	___ + 9 = 12	___ + 9 = 10	5 + ___ = 11
14.	___ + 1 = 10	___ + 2 = 11	2 + ___ = 12	8 + ___ = 14
15.	___ + 3 = 13	___ + 1 = 10	___ + 4 = 11	6 + ___ = 12

Name _____ Date _____

ADDITION FACTS 2

DIRECTIONS: Add from top to bottom. Check your answers by adding from bottom to top.

1. 6   8   2   9   6   7   6   5   4   3   8   7   3
    9   7   4   5   6   4   8   5   9   8   2   6   9

2. 3   7   8   3   4   5   8   7   6   5   8   7   2
    9   6   2   8   9   9   6   4   6   5   4   7   9

3. 9   3   9   7   6   8   3   7   5   8   5   4   1
    2   7   4   5   8   4   8   6   9   6   5   6   9

4. 4   7   8   6   2   6   3   7   5   5   7   6   9
    9   7   2   7   9   6   8   7   6   5   3   7   1

5. 2   6   8   5   6   7   4   5   4   8   8   3   3
    9   7   4   5   8   4   8   5   9   6   5   7   9

6. 4   7   8   3   5   5   4   7   6   9   8   7   1
    6   6   4   8   9   5   8   4   4   5   5   7   9

2A. DIRECTIONS: Fill in the blanks. **Hint.** To find the missing numeral, subtract the smaller numeral from the larger numeral.

Example: 3 + __ = 10 Solution: 10 - 3 = 7 So: 3 + 7 = 10

1. 12 + __ = 12	7 + __ = 14	__ + 9 = 10	4 + __ = 13
2. 5 + __ = 13	__ + 8 = 11	6 + __ = 12	__ + 11 = 14
3. __ + 10 = 10	5 + __ = 12	__ + 7 = 13	__ + 9 = 11
4. 5 + __ = 14	__ + 1 = 13	__ + 2 = 11	__ + 9 = 12
5. __ + 7 = 11	5 + __ = 10	__ + 1 = 14	__ + 2 = 13
6. __ + 9 = 12	7 + __ = 13	3 + __ = 14	__ + 9 = 12
7. 5 + __ = 14	__ + 1 = 12	__ + 2 = 13	3 + __ = 10
8. __ + 1 = 10	__ + 2 = 11	5 + __ = 12	__ + 2 = 13
9. 0 + __ = 13	__ + 0 = 12	11 + __ = 11	__ + 0 = 14
10. __ + 0 = 10	__ + 4 = 11	__ + 7 = 12	0 + __ = 11
11. 1 + __ = 11	__ + 1 = 10	__ + 3 = 12	7 + __ = 14
12. 8 + __ = 14	5 + __ = 13	__ + 9 = 11	__ + 10 = 10
13. 12 + __ = 14	__ + 10 = 12	4 + __ = 11	10 + __ = 11
14. __ + 1 = 10	__ + 12 = 14	12 + __ = 13	1 + __ = 12
15. __ + 3 = 12	__ + 10 = 14	__ + 4 = 11	6 + __ = 10

Nettie Whitney Bailey

Name _____ Date _____

ADDITION FACTS 3

DIRECTIONS: Add from top to bottom. Check your work by adding from bottom to top.

1.	7	6	8	6	6	7	8	6	8	5	8	9	6
	8	7	6	9	5	5	7	5	6	7	5	6	8

2.	3	7	8	3	4	7	4	7	6	5	8	6	9
	8	7	7	7	6	8	9	8	7	9	6	9	5

3.	6	6	9	8	6	7	2	5	5	9	8	2	9
	9	8	4	7	8	8	9	5	6	6	7	9	6

4.	7	6	8	9	6	7	4	5	9	3	8	7	7
	8	4	7	5	9	7	7	6	6	7	7	7	8

5.	3	7	8	3	4	9	7	7	6	5	7	6	2
	8	7	7	7	6	6	8	3	6	5	8	9	8

6.	6	6	9	4	7	7	2	5	8	9	3	6	9
	9	4	2	7	8	3	9	5	7	6	7	9	2

3A. DIRECTIONS: Fill in the blanks. **Hint.** To find the missing numeral, subtract the smaller numeral from the larger numeral.

Example: 3 + __ = 10 Solution: 10 - 3 = 7 So: 3 + 7 = 10.

1.	5 + __ = 12	__ + 8 = 13	6 + __ = 15	__ + 11 = 14
2.	__ + 10 = 11	5 + __ = 14	__ + 7 = 10	__ + 9 = 15
3.	5 + __ = 13	__ + 1 = 10	__ + 2 = 12	__ + 9 = 14
4.	4 + __ = 13	5 + __ = 12	__ + 1 = 11	__ + 2 = 15
5.	__ + 9 = 12	7 + __ = 14	3 + __ = 10	__ + 9 = 13
6.	5 + __ = 15	__ + 1 = 11	__ + 2 = 14	3 + __ = 12
7.	__ + 1 = 14	__ + 2 = 13	3 + __ = 15	__ + 2 = 11
8.	5 + __ = 12	__ + 1 = 15	6 + __ = 14	__ + 9 = 10
9.	__ + 1 = 15	__ + 2 = 10	__ + 7 = 12	1 + __ = 14
10.	10 + __ = 10	__ + 10 = 12	__ + 3 = 11	7 + __ = 15
11.	8 + __ = 11	5 + __ = 14	__ + 9 = 10	__ + 10 = 13
12.	12 + __ = 13	__ + 9 = 10	4 + __ = 15	5 + __ = 12
13.	__ + 1 = 15	__ + 2 = 15	2 + __ = 11	8 + __ = 14
14.	__ + 3 = 15	__ + 10 = 10	__ + 4 = 12	6 + __ = 13
15.	11 + __ = 14	7 + __ = 11	__ + 0 = 15	1 + __ = 12

Name _____ Date _____

ADDITION FACTS 4

4a. DIRECTIONS: Add from top to bottom. Check your work by adding from bottom to top.

1. 7   6   8   5   8   7   4   5   4   8   8   7   9
  <u>9</u>   <u>7</u>   <u>4</u>   <u>5</u>   <u>8</u>   <u>8</u>   <u>7</u>   <u>5</u>   <u>9</u>   <u>8</u>   <u>7</u>   <u>5</u>   <u>7</u>

2. 9   7   8   7   5   5   8   6   3   7   8   6   2
  <u>7</u>   <u>6</u>   <u>8</u>   <u>8</u>   <u>9</u>   <u>5</u>   <u>8</u>   <u>4</u>   <u>7</u>   <u>9</u>   <u>4</u>   <u>9</u>   <u>9</u>

3. 4   9   8   4   9   6   7   6   9   7   8   7   5
  <u>9</u>   <u>7</u>   <u>8</u>   <u>8</u>   <u>3</u>   <u>6</u>   <u>9</u>   <u>8</u>   <u>5</u>   <u>7</u>   <u>8</u>   <u>9</u>   <u>5</u>

4. 8   7   9   7   8   7   4   7   7   8   3   5   9
  <u>8</u>   <u>7</u>   <u>4</u>   <u>9</u>   <u>8</u>   <u>3</u>   <u>7</u>   <u>5</u>   <u>9</u>   <u>8</u>   <u>7</u>   <u>7</u>   <u>7</u>

5. 6   7   8   7   5   5   8   6   9   3   8   7   5
  <u>9</u>   <u>9</u>   <u>8</u>   <u>4</u>   <u>6</u>   <u>5</u>   <u>8</u>   <u>4</u>   <u>7</u>   <u>9</u>   <u>8</u>   <u>9</u>   <u>7</u>

6. 7   6   8   4   9   6   7   8   9   7   5   2   8
  <u>9</u>   <u>8</u>   <u>8</u>   <u>9</u>   <u>7</u>   <u>4</u>   <u>7</u>   <u>8</u>   <u>3</u>   <u>9</u>   <u>7</u>   <u>9</u>   <u>8</u>

4A. DIRECTIONS: Fill in the blanks. **Hint**. To find the missing numeral, subtract the smaller numeral from the larger numeral.

Example: 3 + __ = 10 Solution: 10 - 3 = 7 So: 3 + 7 = 10

1.	5 + __ = 12	__ + 8 = 13	6 + __ = 15	__ + 11 = 16
2.	__ + 10 = 11	5 + __ = 14	__ + 7 = 10	__ + 9 = 15
3.	5 + __ = 16	__ + 1 = 10	__ + 2 = 12	__ + 9 = 14
4.	4 + __ = 13	5 + __ = 12	__ + 1 = 11	__ + 2 = 15
5.	__ + 9 = 12	7 + __ = 16	3 + __ = 10	__ + 9 = 13
6.	5 + __ = 15	__ + 1 = 11	__ + 2 = 14	3 + __ = 12
7.	__ + 1 = 14	__ + 2 = 13	3 + __ = 15	__ + 2 = 11
8.	5 + __ = 12	__ + 1 = 15	6 + __ = 16	__ + 9 = 10
9.	__ + 1 = 16	__ + 2 = 10	__ + 7 = 12	1 + __ = 14
10.	10 + __ = 10	__ + 10 = 12	__ + 3 = 11	7 + __ = 16
11.	8 + __ = 11	5 + __ = 14	__ + 9 = 10	__ + 10 = 13
12.	12 + __ = 13	__ + 9 = 10	4 + __ = 15	5 + __ = 12
13.	__ + 1 = 15	__ + 2 = 16	2 + __ = 11	8 + __ = 14
14.	__ + 3 = 15	__ + 10 = 10	__ + 4 = 12	6 + __ = 13
15.	11 + __ = 14	7 + __ = 11	__ + 0 = 16	1 + __ = 12

Name _____ Date _____

ADDITION FACTS 5

DIRECTIONS: Add from top to bottom. Check your answers by adding from bottom to top.

1. 8	5	7	9	9	7	4	5	4	3	8	7	8
9	7	4	5	6	6	8	5	6	8	5	8	9
2. 3	7	8	3	4	5	4	7	6	5	8	7	2
8	6	8	7	6	5	9	4	6	5	8	7	9
3. 2	6	9	4	2	7	9	5	5	9	3	8	9
8	7	1	8	8	6	8	8	6	4	9	9	3
4. 7	6	8	8	8	9	8	5	6	8	9	7	8
9	7	4	5	6	6	8	5	6	8	8	8	9
5. 2	4	6	8	7	5	8	9	5	8	8	5	7
8	6	8	7	6	5	9	8	6	5	8	7	3
6. 5	9	8	7	9	4	8	7	6	9	3	8	6
8	7	9	8	8	6	9	7	6	8	7	9	6

5A. DIRECTIONS: Fill in the blanks. **Hint.** To find the missing numeral, subtract the smaller numeral from the larger numeral.

Example: 3 + __ = 10 Solution: 10 - 3 = 7 So: 3 + 7 = 10

1.	13 + __ = 17	7 + __ = 15	__ + 9 = 13	4 + __ = 11
2.	5 + __ = 12	__ + 6 = 17	6 + __ = 16	__ + 10 = 10
3.	__ + 10 = 13	5 + __ = 10	__ + 7 = 17	__ + 9 = 16
4.	5 + __ = 17	__ + 1 = 13	__ + 2 = 10	__ + 9 = 12
5.	8 + __ = 17	5 + __ = 11	__ + 1 = 17	__ + 2 = 15
6.	__ + 9 = 10	7 + __ = 12	3 + __ = 17	__ + 9 = 16
7.	5 + __ = 12	__ + 10 = 17	__ + 0 = 11	3 + __ = 13
8.	__ + 15 = 15	__ + 2 = 17	3 + __ = 12	__ + 2 = 14
9.	17 + __ = 17	__ + 1 = 11	6 + __ = 13	__ + 9 = 17
10.	__ + 0 = 10	15 + __ = 17	__ + 4 = 14	14 + __ = 14
11.	11 + __ = 13	__ + 12 = 17	__ + 3 = 11	7 + __ = 16
12.	8 + __ = 14	7 + __ = 17	__ + 0 = 16	__ + 10 = 15
13.	11 + __ = 11	__ + 3 = 17	__ + 9 = 17	5 + __ = 12
14.	__ + 1 = 16	__ + 2 = 13	2 + __ = 10	14 + __ = 17
15.	__ + 3 = 13	__ + 11 = 17	__ + 4 = 15	6 + __ = 10

Name _____ Date _____

ADDITION FACTS 6

DIRECTIONS: Add from top to bottom. Check your answers by adding from bottom to top.

1. 9   5   7   9   9   7   4   5   9   3   8   7   8
     9   7   4   5   6   6   8   5   9   8   5   8   9

2. 3   7   8   3   9   5   4   7   6   5   8   7   9
     8   6   8   7   9   5   9   4   6   5   8   7   9

3. 2   6   9   4   2   7   9   5   5   9   3   8   9
     8   7   9   8   8   6   8   8   6   9   9   9   9

4. 7   6   8   8   8   9   8   5   6   8   9   7   9
     9   7   4   5   6   9   8   5   6   8   8   8   9

5. 9   4   6   8   7   5   9   9   5   8   8   5   7
     9   6   8   7   6   5   9   8   6   5   8   7   3

6. 5   9   8   7   9   4   9   7   6   9   3   9   6
     8   9   9   8   8   6   9   7   6   8   7   9   7

6A. DIRECTIONS: Fill in the blanks. **Hint**. To find the missing numeral, subtract the smaller numeral from the larger numeral.

Example: 3 + __ = 10 Solution: 10 - 3 = 7 So: 3 + 7 = 10

1.	12 + __ = 18	7 + __ = 15	__ + 9 = 14	4 + __ = 16
2.	5 + __ = 13	__ + 8 = 17	6 + __ = 18	__ + 11 = 11
3.	__ + 10 = 18	5 + __ = 17	__ + 7 = 13	__ + 9 = 12
4.	5 + __ = 14	__ + 1 = 18	__ + 2 = 16	__ + 9 = 15
5.	3 + __ = 14	5 + __ = 12	__ + 1 = 10	__ + 2 = 18
6.	__ + 9 = 16	7 + __ = 18	3 + __ = 10	__ + 9 = 13
7.	5 + __ = 17	__ + 1 = 11	__ + 3 = 18	3 + __ = 15
8.	__ + 6 = 16	__ + 3 = 10	9 + __ = 18	__ + 6 = 18
9.	5 + __ = 14	__ + 1 = 12	__ + 9 = 18	__ + 9 = 17
10.	__ + 7 = 18	__ + 2 = 13	11 + __ = 18	15 + __ = 18
11.	13 + __ = 18	__ + 10 = 15	__ + 10 = 18	7 + __ = 11
12.	8 + __ = 18	5 + __ = 14	__ + 9 = 16	__ + 12 = 18
13.	12 + __ = 13	__ + 9 = 10	__ + 12 = 17	5 + __ = 18
14.	__ + 1 = 16	__ + 11 = 18	2 + __ = 17	8 + __ = 15
15.	__ + 3 = 14	__ + 10 = 11	__ + 4 = 18	6 + __ = 18

ADDITION TABLE

Give the ADDITION TABLE to each student that does not KNOW his/her number facts through 18, students who are still counting on fingers, drawing circles or sticks, or doing mental math to figure out answers. Teach them how to use it and direct them to use it when solving problems. This will enable them to get correct answers as well as learn the addition facts.

Name _____

ADDITION TABLE

+	1	2	3	4	5	6	7	8	9
1	2	3	4	5	6	7	8	9	10
2	3	4	5	6	7	8	9	10	11
3	4	5	6	7	8	9	10	11	12
4	5	6	7	8	9	10	11	12	13
5	6	7	8	9	10	11	12	13	14
6	7	8	9	10	11	12	13	14	15
7	8	9	10	11	12	13	14	15	16
8	9	10	11	12	13	14	15	16	17
9	10	11	12	13	14	15	16	17	18

Name _____ Date _____

ADDITION / MULTIPLICATION 1

DIRECTIONS: Find the sums and products.

1. $0 \times 0 =$ ___

2. $0 =$ ___ $= 0 \times 1 =$ ___

3. $0 + 0 =$ ___ $= 0 \times 2 =$ ___

4. $0 + 0 =$ ___ $+ 0 =$ ___ $= 0 \times 3 =$ ___

5. $0 + 0 =$ ___ $+ 0 =$ ___ $+ 0 =$ ___ $= 0 \times 4 =$ ___

6. $0 + 0 =$ ___ $+ 0 =$ ___ $+ 0$ ___ $= + 0 =$ ___ $= 0 \times 5 =$ ___

7. $0 + 0 =$ ___ $+ 0 =$ ___ $+ 0 =$ ___ $+ 0 =$ ___ $+ 0 =$ ___ $= 0 \times 6 =$ ___

8. $0 + 0 =$ ___ $+ 0 =$ ___ $+ 0 =$ ___ $+ 0 =$ ___ $+ 0 =$ ___ $+ 0 =$ ___ $= 0$

    $\times 7 =$ ___

9. $0 + 0 =$ ___ $+ 0 =$ ___ $+ 0 =$ ___ $+ 0 =$ ___ $+ 0 =$ ___ $+ 0 =$ ___ $+ 0$

    $=$ ___ $= 0 \times 8 =$ ___

10. $0 + 0 =$ ___ $+ 0 =$ ___ $+ 0$ ___ $+ 0 =$ ___ $+ 0 =$ ___ $+ 0 =$ ___ $+ 0 =$

    ___ $+ 0 =$ ___ $= 0 \times 9 =$ ___

11.   0 + 0 = ___ + 0 = ___ + 0 = ___ + 0 = ___ + 0 = ___ + 0 = ___ + 0

= ___ + 0 = ___ + 0 = ___ = 0 x 10 = ___

12.   0 + 0 = ___ + 0 = ___ + 0 = ___ + 0 = ___ + 0 = ___ + 0 = ___ + 0

= ___ + 0 ___ + 0 = ___ + 0 = ___ = 0 x 11 = ___

13.   0 = ___ + 0 = ___ + 0 = ___ + 0 = ___ + 0 = ___ + 0 = ___ + 0 =

___ + 0 = ___ + 0 = ___ + 0 = ___ + 0 = ___ + 0 = ___ = 0 x 12 =

___

0 x 0 = ___ 1 x 0 = ___ 2 x 0 = ___ 3 x 0 = ___ 4 x 0 = ___ 5 x 0 = ___ 6 x 0 = ___ 7 x 0 = ___ 8 x 0 = ___ 9 x 0 = ___ 10 x 0 = ___ 11 x 0 = ___ 12 x 0 = ___	0 x 0 = ___ 1 x 0 = ___ 2 x 0 = ___ 3 x 0 = ___ 4 x 0 = ___ 5 x 0 = ___ 6 x 0 = ___ 7 x 0 = ___ 8 x 0 = ___ 9 x 0 = ___ 10 x 0 = ___ 11 x 0 = ___ 12 x 0 = ___
0 x 0 = ___ 1 x 0 = ___ 2 x 0 = ___ 3 x 0 = ___ 4 x 0 = ___ 5 x 0 = ___ 6 x 0 = ___ 7 x 0 = ___ 8 x 0 = ___ 9 x 0 = ___ 10 x 0 = ___ 11 x 0 = ___ 12 x 0 = ___	0 x 0 = ___ 1 x 0 = ___ 2 x 0 = ___ 3 x 0 = ___ 4 x 0 = ___ 5 x 0 = ___ 6 x 0 = ___ 7 x 0 = ___ 8 x 0 = ___ 9 x 0 = ___ 10 x 0 = ___ 11 x 0 = ___ 12 x 0 = ___

Name _____ Date _____

ADDITION/MULTIPLICATION 2

DIRECTIONS: Find the sums and products.

1. $1 \times 0 = $ ___

2. $1 = $ ___ $ = 1 \times 1 = $ ___

3. $1 + 1 = $ ___ $ = 1 \times 2 = $ ___

4. $1 + 1 = $ ___ $ + 1 = $ ___ $ = 1 \times 3 = $ ___

5. $1 + 1 = $ ___ $ + 1 = $ ___ $ + 1 = $ ___ $ = 1 \times 4 = $ ___

6. $1 + 1 = $ ___ $ + 1 = $ ___ $ + 1 = $ ___ $ + 1 = $ ___ $ = 1 \times 5 = $ ___

7. $1 + 1 = $ ___ $ + 1 = $ ___ $ + 1 = $ ___ $ + 1 = $ ___ $ + 1 = $ ___ $ = 1 \times 6 = $ ___

8. $1 + 1 = $ ___ $ + 1 = $ ___ $ + 1 = $ ___ $ + 1 = $ ___ $ + 1 = $ ___ $ + 1 = $ ___ $ = 1$

    $\times 7 = $ ___

9. $1 + 1 = $ ___ $ + 1 = $ ___ $ + 1 = $ ___ $ + 1 = $ ___ $ + 1 = $ ___ $ + 1 = $ ___ $ + 1$

    $ = $ ___ $ = 1 \times 8 = $ ___

10. $1 + 1 = $ ___ $ + 1 = $ ___ $ + 1$ ___ $ + 1 = $ ___ $ + 1 = $ ___ $ + 1 = $ ___ $ + 1 = $

    ___ $ + 1 = $ ___ $ = 1 \times 9 = $ ___

11. $1 + 1 = $ ___ $+ 1 = $ ___ $+ 1 = $ ___ $+ 1 = $ ___ $+ 1 = $ ___ $+ 1 = $ ___ $+ 1$

= ___ $+ 1 = $ ___ $+ 1 = $ ___ $= 1 \times 10 = $ ___

12. $1 + 1 = $ ___ $+ 1 = $ ___ $+ 1 = $ ___ $+ 1 = $ ___ $+ 1 = $ ___ $+ 1 = $ ___ $+ 1$

= ___ $+ 1 = $ ___ $+ 1 = $ ___ $+ 1 = $ ___ $= 1 \times 11 = $ ___

13. $1 + 1 = $ ___ $+ 1 = $ ___ $+ 1 = $ ___ $+ 1 = $ ___ $+ 1 = $ ___ $+ 1 = $ ___ $+ 1$

= ___ $+ 1 = $ ___ $+ 1 = $ ___ $+ 1 = $ ___ $+ 1 = $ ___ $1 \times 12 = $ ___

$0 \times 1 = $ ___ $1 \times 1 = $ ___ $2 \times 1 = $ ___ $3 \times 1 = $ ___ $4 \times 1 = $ ___ $5 \times 1 = $ ___ $6 \times 1 = $ ___ $7 \times 1 = $ ___ $8 \times 1 = $ ___ $9 \times 1 = $ ___ $10 \times 1 = $ ___ $11 \times 1 = $ ___ $12 \times 1 = $ ___	$0 \times 1 = $ ___ $1 \times 1 = $ ___ $2 \times 1 = $ ___ $3 \times 1 = $ ___ $4 \times 1 = $ ___ $5 \times 1 = $ ___ $6 \times 1 = $ ___ $7 \times 1 = $ ___ $8 \times 1 = $ ___ $9 \times 1 = $ ___ $10 \times 1 = $ ___ $11 \times 1 = $ ___ $12 \times 1 = $ ___
$0 \times 1 = $ ___ $1 \times 1 = $ ___ $2 \times 1 = $ ___ $3 \times 1 = $ ___ $4 \times 1 = $ ___ $5 \times 1 = $ ___ $6 \times 1 = $ ___ $7 \times 1 = $ ___ $8 \times 1 = $ ___ $9 \times 1 = $ ___ $10 \times 1 = $ ___ $11 \times 1 = $ ___ $12 \times 1 = $ ___	$0 \times 1 = $ ___ $1 \times 1 = $ ___ $2 \times 1 = $ ___ $3 \times 1 = $ ___ $4 \times 1 = $ ___ $5 \times 1 = $ ___ $6 \times 1 = $ ___ $7 \times 1 = $ ___ $8 \times 1 = $ ___ $9 \times 1 = $ ___ $10 \times 1 = $ ___ $11 \times 1 = $ ___ $12 \times 1 = $ ___

Name _____ Date _____

ADDITION/MULTIPLICATION 3

DIRECTIONS: Find the sums and products.

1. $2 \times 0 =$ ___

2. $2 =$ ___ $= 2 \times 1 =$ ___

3. $2 + 2 =$ ___ $= 2 \times 2 =$ ___

4. $2 + 2 =$ ___ $+ 2 =$ ___ $= 2 \times 3 =$ ___

5. $2 + 2 =$ ___ $+ 2 =$ ___ $+ 2 =$ ___ $= 2 \times 4 =$ ___

6. $2 + 2 =$ ___ $+ 2 =$ ___ $+ 2 =$ ___ $+ 2 =$ ___ $= 2 \times 5 =$ ___

7. $2 + 2 =$ ___ $+ 2 =$ ___ $+ 2 =$ ___ $+ 2 =$ ___ $+ 2 =$ ___ $= 2 \times 6 =$

    ___

8. $2 + 2 =$ ___ $+ 2 =$ ___ $+ 2 =$ ___ $+ 2 =$ ___ $+ 2 =$ ___ $+ 2 =$ ___

    $= 2 \times 7 =$ ___

9. $2 + 2 =$ ___ $+ 2 =$ ___ $+ 2 =$ ___ $+ 2 =$ ___ $+ 2 =$ ___ $+ 2 =$ ___

    $+ 2 =$ ___ $= 2 \times 8 =$ ___

10. $2 + 2 =$ ___ $+ 2 =$ ___ $+ 2$ ___ $+ 2 =$ ___ $+ 2 =$ ___ $+ 2 =$ ___ $+$

    $2 =$ ___ $+ 2 =$ ___ $= 2 \times 9 =$ ___

11. 2 + 2 = ___ + 2 = ___ + 2 = ___ + 2 = ___ + 2 = ___ + 2 = ___

+ 2 = ___ + 2 = ___ + 2 = ___ = 2 x 10 = ___

12. 2 + 2 = ___ + 2 = ___ + 2 = ___ + 2 = ___ + 2 = ___ + 2 = ___

+ 2 = ___ + 2 = ___ + 2 = ___ + 2 = ___ = 2 x 11 = ___

13. 2 + 2 = ___ + 2 = ___ + 2 = ___ + 2 = ___ + 2 = ___ + 2 = ___

+ 2 = ___ + 2 = ___ + 2 = ___ + 2 = ___ + 2 = ___ = 2 x 12 =

___

0 x 2 = ___ 1 x 2 = ___ 2 x 2 = ___ 3 x 2 = ___ 4 x 2 = ___ 5 x 2 = ___ 6 x 2 = ___ 7 x 2 = ___ 8 x 2 = ___ 9 x 2 = ___ 10 x 2 = ___ 11 x 2 = ___ 12 x 2 = ___	0 x 2 = ___ 1 x 2 = ___ 2 x 2 = ___ 3 x 2 = ___ 4 x 2 = ___ 5 x 2 = ___ 6 x 2 = ___ 7 x 2 = ___ 8 x 2 = ___ 9 x 2 = ___ 10 x 2 = ___ 11 x 2 = ___ 12 x 2 = ___
0 x 2 = ___ 1 x 2 = ___ 2 x 2 = ___ 3 x 2 = ___ 4 x 2 = ___ 5 x 2 = ___ 6 x 2 = ___ 7 x 2 = ___ 8 x 2 = ___ 9 x 2 = ___ 10 x 2 = ___ 11 x 2 = ___ 12 x 2 = ___	0 x 2 = ___ 1 x 2 = ___ 2 x 2 = ___ 3 x 2 = ___ 4 x 2 = ___ 5 x 2 = ___ 6 x 2 = ___ 7 x 2 = ___ 8 x 2 = ___ 9 x 2 = ___ 10 x 2 = ___ 11 x 2 = ___ 12 x 2 = ___

Name _____ Date _____

ADDITION/MULTIPLICATION 4

DIRECTIONS: Find the sums and products.

1. $3 \times 0 =$ ___

2. $3 =$ ___ $= 3 \times 1 =$ ___

3. $3 + 3 =$ ___ $= 3 \times 2 =$ ___

4. $3 + 3 =$ ___ $+ 3 =$ ___ $= 3 \times 3 =$ ___

5. $3 + 3 =$ ___ $+ 3 =$ ___ $+ 3 =$ ___ $= 3 \times 4 =$ ___

6. $3 + 3 =$ ___ $+ 3 =$ ___ $+ 3 =$ ___ $+ 3 =$ ___ $= 3 \times 5 =$ ___

7. $3 + 3 =$ ___ $+ 3 =$ ___ $+ 3 =$ ___ $+ 3 =$ ___ $+ 3 =$ ___ $= 3 \times 6 =$

    ___

8. $3 + 3 =$ ___ $+ 3 =$ ___ $+ 3 =$ ___ $+ 3 =$ ___ $+ 3 =$ ___ $+ 3 =$ ___

    $= 3 \times 7 =$ ___

9. $3 + 3 =$ ___ $+ 3 =$ ___ $+ 3 =$ ___ $+ 3 =$ ___ $+ 3 =$ ___ $+ 3 =$ ___

    $+ 3 =$ ___ $= 3 \times 8 =$ ___

10. $3 + 3 =$ ___ $+ 3 =$ ___ $+ 3$ ___ $+ 3 =$ ___ $+ 3 =$ ___ $+ 3 =$ ___ $+$

    $3 =$ ___ $+ 3 =$ ___ $= 3 \times 9 =$ ___

11. $3 + 3 =$ ___ $+ 3 =$ ___ $+ 3 =$ ___ $+ 3 =$ ___ $+ 3 =$ ___ $+ 3 =$ ___

$+ 3 =$ ___ $+ 3 =$ ___ $+ 3 =$ ___ $= 3 \times 10 =$ ___

12. $3 + 3 =$ ___ $+ 3 =$ ___ $+ 3 =$ ___ $+ 3 =$ ___ $+ 3 =$ ___ $+ 3 =$ ___

$+ 3 =$ ___ $+ 3 =$ ___ $+ 3 =$ ___ $+ 3 =$ ___ $= 3 \times 11 =$ ___

13. $3 + 3 =$ ___ $+ 3 =$ ___ $+ 3 =$ ___ $+ 3 =$ ___ $+ 3 =$ ___ $+ 3 =$ ___

$+ 3 =$ ___ $+ 3 =$ ___ $+ 3 =$ ___ $+ 3 =$ ___ $+ 3 =$ ___ $= 3 \times 12 =$

___

$0 \times 3 =$ ___ $1 \times 3 =$ ___ $2 \times 3 =$ ___ $3 \times 3 =$ ___ $4 \times 3 =$ ___ $5 \times 3 =$ ___ $6 \times 3 =$ ___ $7 \times 3 =$ ___ $8 \times 3 =$ ___ $9 \times 3 =$ ___ $10 \times 3 =$ ___ $11 \times 3 =$ ___ $12 \times 3 =$ ___	$0 \times 3 =$ ___ $1 \times 3 =$ ___ $2 \times 3 =$ ___ $3 \times 3 =$ ___ $4 \times 3 =$ ___ $5 \times 3 =$ ___ $6 \times 3 =$ ___ $7 \times 3 =$ ___ $8 \times 3 =$ ___ $9 \times 3 =$ ___ $10 \times 3 =$ ___ $11 \times 3 =$ ___ $12 \times 3 =$ ___
$0 \times 3 =$ ___ $1 \times 3 =$ ___ $2 \times 3 =$ ___ $3 \times 3 =$ ___ $4 \times 3 =$ ___ $5 \times 3 =$ ___ $6 \times 3 =$ ___ $7 \times 3 =$ ___ $8 \times 3 =$ ___ $9 \times 3 =$ ___ $10 \times 3 =$ ___ $11 \times 3 =$ ___ $12 \times 3 =$ ___	$0 \times 3 =$ ___ $1 \times 3 =$ ___ $2 \times 3 =$ ___ $3 \times 3 =$ ___ $4 \times 3 =$ ___ $5 \times 3 =$ ___ $6 \times 3 =$ ___ $7 \times 3 =$ ___ $8 \times 3 =$ ___ $9 \times 3 =$ ___ $10 \times 3 =$ ___ $11 \times 3 =$ ___ $12 \times 3 =$ ___

Name _____ Date _____

ADDITION/MULTIPLICATION 5

DIRECTIONS: Find the sums and products.

1. $4 \times 0 =$ ___

2. $4 =$ ___ $= 4 \times 1 =$ ___

3. $4 + 4 =$ ___ $= 4 \times 2 =$ ___

4. $4 + 4 =$ ___ $+ 4 =$ ___ $= 4 \times 3 =$ ___

5. $4 + 4 =$ ___ $+ 4 =$ ___ $+ 4 =$ ___ $= 4 \times 4 =$ ___

6. $4 + 4 =$ ___ $+ 4 =$ ___ $+ 4 =$ ___ $+ 4 =$ ___ $= 4 \times 5 =$ ___

7. $4 + 4 =$ ___ $+ 4 =$ ___ $+ 4 =$ ___ $+ 4 =$ ___ $+ 4 =$ ___ $= 4 \times 6 =$ ___

8. $4 + 4 =$ ___ $+ 4 =$ ___ $+ 4 =$ ___ $+ 4 =$ ___ $+ 4 =$ ___ $+ 4 =$ ___ $= 4$

      $\times 7 =$ ___

9. $4 + 4 =$ ___ $+ 4 =$ ___ $+ 4 =$ ___ $+ 4 =$ ___ $+ 4 =$ ___ $+ 4 =$ ___ $+ 4$

      $=$ ___ $= 4 \times 8 =$ ___

10. $4 + 4 =$ ___ $+ 4 =$ ___ $+ 4$ ___ $+ 4 =$ ___ $+ 4 =$ ___ $+ 4 =$ ___ $+ 4 =$

      ___ $+ 4 =$ ___ $= 4 \times 9 =$ ___

11. 4 + 4 = ___ + 4 = ___ + 4 = ___ + 4 = ___ + 4 = ___ + 4 = ___ + 4

= ___ + 4 = ___ + 4 = ___ = 4 x 10 = ___

12. 4 + 4 = ___ + 4 = ___ + 4 = ___ + 4 = ___ + 4 = ___ + 4 = ___ + 4

= ___ + 4 = ___ + 4 = ___ + 4 = ___ = 4 x 11 = ___

13. 4 + 4 = ___ + 4 = ___ + 4 = ___ + 4 = ___ + 4 = ___ + 4 = ___ + 4

= ___ + 4 = ___ + 4 = ___ + 4 = ___ + 4 = ___ = 4 x 12 = ___

0 x 4 = ___ 1 x 4 = ___ 2 x 4 = ___ 3 x 4 = ___ 4 x 4 = ___ 5 x 4 = ___ 6 x 4 = ___ 7 x 4 = ___ 8 x 4 = ___ 9 x 4 = ___ 10 x 4 = ___ 11 x 4 = ___ 12 x 4 = ___	0 x 4 = ___ 1 x 4 = ___ 2 x 4 = ___ 3 x 4 = ___ 4 x 4 = ___ 5 x 4 = ___ 6 x 4 = ___ 7 x 4 = ___ 8 x 4 = ___ 9 x 4 = ___ 10 x 4 = ___ 11 x 4 = ___ 12 x 4 = ___
0 x 4 = ___ 1 x 4 = ___ 2 x 4 = ___ 3 x 4 = ___ 4 x 4 = ___ 5 x 4 = ___ 6 x 4 = ___ 7 x 4 = ___ 8 x 4 = ___ 9 x 4 = ___ 10 x 4 = ___ 11 x 4 = ___ 12 x 4 = ___	0 x 4 = ___ 1 x 4 = ___ 2 x 4 = ___ 3 x 4 = ___ 4 x 4 = ___ 5 x 4 = ___ 6 x 4 = ___ 7 x 4 = ___ 8 x 4 = ___ 9 x 4 = ___ 10 x 4 = ___ 11 x 4 = ___ 12 x 4 = ___

Name _____ Date _____

ADDITION/MULTIPLICATION 6

DIRECTIONS: Find the sums and products.

1. $5 \times 0 =$ ___

2. $5 =$ ___ $= 5 \times 1 =$ ___

3. $5 + 5 =$ ___ $= 5 \times 2 =$ ___

4. $5 + 5 =$ ___ $+ 5 =$ ___ $= 5 \times 3 =$ ___

5. $5 + 5 =$ ___ $+ 5 =$ ___ $+ 5 =$ ___ $= 5 \times 4 =$ ___

6. $5 + 5 =$ ___ $+ 5 =$ ___ $+ 5 =$ ___ $+ 5 =$ ___ $= 5 \times 5 =$ ___

7. $5 + 5 =$ ___ $+ 5 =$ ___ $+ 5 =$ ___ $+ 5 =$ ___ $+ 5 =$ ___ $= 5 \times 6 =$

   ___

8. $5 + 5 =$ ___ $+ 5 =$ ___ $+ 5 =$ ___ $+ 5 =$ ___ $+ 5 =$ ___ $+ 5 =$ ___

   $= 5 \times 7 =$ ___

9. $5 + 5 =$ ___ $+ 5 =$ ___ $+ 5 =$ ___ $+ 5 =$ ___ $+ 5 =$ ___ $+ 5 =$ ___

   $+ 5 =$ ___ $= 5 \times 8 =$ ___

10. $5 + 5 =$ ___ $+ 5 =$ ___ $+ 5$ ___ $+ 5 =$ ___ $+ 5 =$ ___ $+ 5 =$ ___ $+$

    $5 =$ ___ $+ 5 =$ ___ $= 5 \times 9 =$ ___

11. $5 + 5 =$ ___ $+ 5 =$ ___ $+ 5 =$ ___ $+ 5 =$ ___ $+ 5 =$ ___ $+ 5 =$ ___

      $+ 5 =$ ___ $+ 5 =$ ___ $+ 5 =$ ___ $= 5 \times 10 =$ ___

12. $5 + 5 =$ ___ $+ 5 =$ ___ $+ 5 =$ ___ $+ 5 =$ ___ $+ 5 =$ ___ $+ 5 =$ ___

      $+ 5 =$ ___ $+ 5 =$ ___ $+ 5 =$ ___ $+ 5 =$ ___ $= 5 \times 11 =$ ___

13. $5 + 5 =$ ___ $+ 5 =$ ___ $+ 5 =$ ___ $+ 5 =$ ___ $+ 5 =$ ___ $+ 5 =$ ___

      $+ 5 =$ ___ $+ 5 =$ ___ $+ 5 =$ ___ $+ 5 =$ ___ $+ 5 =$ ___ $= 5 \times 12 =$

      ___

$0 \times 5 =$ ___ $1 \times 5 =$ ___ $2 \times 5 =$ ___ $3 \times 5 =$ ___ $4 \times 5 =$ ___ $5 \times 5 =$ ___ $6 \times 5 =$ ___ $7 \times 5 =$ ___ $8 \times 5 =$ ___ $9 \times 5 =$ ___ $10 \times 5 =$ ___ $11 \times 5 =$ ___ $12 \times 5 =$ ___	$0 \times 5 =$ ___ $1 \times 5 =$ ___ $2 \times 5 =$ ___ $3 \times 5 =$ ___ $4 \times 5 =$ ___ $5 \times 5 =$ ___ $6 \times 5 =$ ___ $7 \times 5 =$ ___ $8 \times 5 =$ ___ $9 \times 5 =$ ___ $10 \times 5 =$ ___ $11 \times 5 =$ ___ $12 \times 5 =$ ___
$0 \times 5 =$ ___ $1 \times 5 =$ ___ $2 \times 5 =$ ___ $3 \times 5 =$ ___ $4 \times 5 =$ ___ $5 \times 5 =$ ___ $6 \times 5 =$ ___ $7 \times 5 =$ ___ $8 \times 5 =$ ___ $9 \times 5 =$ ___ $10 \times 5 =$ ___ $11 \times 5 =$ ___ $12 \times 5 =$ ___	$0 \times 5 =$ ___ $1 \times 5 =$ ___ $2 \times 5 =$ ___ $3 \times 5 =$ ___ $4 \times 5 =$ ___ $5 \times 5 =$ ___ $6 \times 5 =$ ___ $7 \times 5 =$ ___ $8 \times 5 =$ ___ $9 \times 5 =$ ___ $10 \times 5 =$ ___ $11 \times 5 =$ ___ $12 \times 5 =$ ___

Name _____ Date _____

ADDITION/MULTIPLICATION 7

DIRECTIONS: Find the sums and products.

1.　$6 \times 0 =$ ___

2.　$6 =$ ___ $= 6 \times 1 =$ ___

3.　$6 + 6 =$ ___ $= 6 \times 2 =$ ___

4.　$6 + 6 =$ ___ $+ 6 =$ ___ $= 6 \times 3 =$ ___

5.　$6 + 6 =$ ___ $+ 6 =$ ___ $+ 6 =$ ___ $= 6 \times 4 =$ ___

6.　$6 + 6 =$ ___ $+ 6 =$ ___ $+ 6 =$ ___ $+ 6 =$ ___ $= 6 \times 5 =$ ___

7.　$6 + 6 =$ ___ $+ 6 =$ ___ $+ 6 =$ ___ $+ 6 =$ ___ $+ 6 =$ ___ $= 6 \times 6 =$

　　___

8.　$6 + 6 =$ ___ $+ 6 =$ ___ $+ 6 =$ ___ $+ 6 =$ ___ $+ 6 =$ ___ $+ 6 =$ ___

　　$= 6 \times 7 =$ ___

9.　$6 + 6 =$ ___ $+ 6 =$ ___ $+ 6 =$ ___ $+ 6 =$ ___ $+ 6 =$ ___ $+ 6 =$ ___

　　$+ 6 =$ ___ $= 6 \times 8 =$ ___

10.　$6 + 6 =$ ___ $+ 6 =$ ___ $+ 6$ ___ $+ 6 =$ ___ $+ 6 =$ ___ $+ 6 =$ ___ $+$

　　$6 =$ ___ $+ 6 =$ ___ $= 6 \times 9 =$ ___

11. 6 + 6 = ___ + 6 = ___ + 6 = ___ + 6 = ___ + 6 = ___ + 6 = ___

+ 6 = ___ + 6 = ___ + 6 = ___ = 6 x 10 = ___

12. 6 + 6 = ___ + 6 = ___ + 6 = ___ + 6 = ___ + 6 = ___ + 6 = ___

+ 6 = ___ + 6 = ___ + 6 = ___ + 6 = ___ = 6 x 11 = ___

13. 6 + 6 = ___ + 6 = ___ + 6 = ___ + 6 = ___ + 6 = ___ + 6 = ___

+ 6 = ___ + 6 = ___ + 6 = ___ + 6 = ___ + 6 = ___ = 6 x 12 =

___

0 x 6 = ___ 1 x 6 = ___ 2 x 6 = ___ 3 x 6 = ___ 4 x 6 = ___ 5 x 6 = ___ 6 x 6 = ___ 7 x 6 = ___ 8 x 6 = ___ 9 x 6 = ___ 10 x 6 = ___ 11 x 6 = ___ 12 x 6 = ___	0 x 6 = ___ 1 x 6 = ___ 2 x 6 = ___ 3 x 6 = ___ 4 x 6 = ___ 5 x 6 = ___ 6 x 6 = ___ 7 x 6 = ___ 8 x 6 = ___ 9 x 6 = ___ 10 x 6 = ___ 11 x 6 = ___ 12 x 6 = ___
0 x 6 = ___ 1 x 6 = ___ 2 x 6 = ___ 3 x 6 = ___ 4 x 6 = ___ 5 x 6 = ___ 6 x 6 = ___ 7 x 6 = ___ 8 x 6 = ___ 9 x 6 = ___ 10 x 6 = ___ 11 x 6 = ___ 12 x 6 = ___	0 x 6 = ___ 1 x 6 = ___ 2 x 6 = ___ 3 x 6 = ___ 4 x 6 = ___ 5 x 6 = ___ 6 x 6 = ___ 7 x 6 = ___ 8 x 6 = ___ 9 x 6 = ___ 10 x 6 = ___ 11 x 6 = ___ 12 x 6 = ___

Name _____ Date _____

ADDITION/MULTIPLICATION 8

DIRECTIONS: Find the sums and products.

1. $7 \times 0 =$ ___

2. $7 =$ ___ $= 7 \times 1 =$ ___

3. $7 + 7 =$ ___ $= 7 \times 2 =$ ___

4. $7 + 7 =$ ___ $+ 7 =$ ___ $= 7 \times 3 =$ ___

    a. $7 + 7 =$ ___ $+ 7 =$ ___ $+ 7 =$ ___ $= 7 \times 4 =$ ___

5. $7 + 7 =$ ___ $+ 7 =$ ___ $+ 7 =$ ___ $+ 7 =$ ___ $= 7 \times 5 =$ ___

6. $7 + 7 =$ ___ $+ 7 =$ ___ $+ 7 =$ ___ $+ 7 =$ ___ $+ 7 =$ ___ $= 7 \times 6 =$ ___

7. $7 + 7 =$ ___ $+ 7 =$ ___ $+ 7 =$ ___ $+ 7 =$ ___ $+ 7 =$ ___ $+ 7 =$ ___ $= 7$

    $\times 7 =$ ___

8. $7 + 7 =$ ___ $+ 7 =$ ___ $+ 7 =$ ___ $+ 7 =$ ___ $+ 7 =$ ___ $+ 7 =$ ___ $+ 7$

    $=$ ___ $= 7 \times 8 =$ ___

9. $7 + 7 =$ ___ $+ 7 =$ ___ $+ 7$ ___ $+ 7 =$ ___ $+ 7 =$ ___ $+ 7 =$ ___ $+ 7 =$

    ___ $+ 7 =$ ___ $= 7 \times 9 =$ ___

10. $7 + 7 = $ ___ $ + 7 = $ ___ $ + 7 = $ ___ $ + 7 = $ ___ $ + 7 = $ ___ $ + 7 = $ ___ $ + 7$

     $ = $ ___ $ + 7 = $ ___ $ + 7 = $ ___ $ = 7 \times 10 = $ ___

11. $7 + 7 = $ ___ $ + 7 = $ ___ $ + 7 = $ ___ $ + 7 = $ ___ $ + 7 = $ ___ $ + 7 = $ ___ $ + 7$

     $ = $ ___ $ + 7 = $ ___ $ + 7 = $ ___ $ + 7 = $ ___ $ = 7 \times 11 = $ ___

12. $7 + 7 = $ ___ $ + 7 = $ ___ $ + 7 = $ ___ $ + 7 = $ ___ $ + 7 = $ ___ $ + 7 = $ ___ $ + 7$

     $ = $ ___ $ + 7 = $ ___ $ + 7 = $ ___ $ + 7 = $ ___ $ + 7 = $ ___ $ = 7 \times 12 = $ ___

$0 \times 7 = $ ___ $1 \times 7 = $ ___ $2 \times 7 = $ ___ $3 \times 7 = $ ___ $4 \times 7 = $ ___ $5 \times 7 = $ ___ $6 \times 7 = $ ___ $7 \times 7 = $ ___ $8 \times 7 = $ ___ $9 \times 7 = $ ___ $10 \times 7 = $ ___ $11 \times 7 = $ ___ $12 \times 7 = $ ___	$0 \times 7 = $ ___ $1 \times 7 = $ ___ $2 \times 7 = $ ___ $3 \times 7 = $ ___ $4 \times 7 = $ ___ $5 \times 7 = $ ___ $6 \times 7 = $ ___ $7 \times 7 = $ ___ $8 \times 7 = $ ___ $9 \times 7 = $ ___ $10 \times 7 = $ ___ $11 \times 7 = $ ___ $12 \times 7 = $ ___
$0 \times 7 = $ ___ $1 \times 7 = $ ___ $2 \times 7 = $ ___ $3 \times 7 = $ ___ $4 \times 7 = $ ___ $5 \times 7 = $ ___ $6 \times 7 = $ ___ $7 \times 7 = $ ___ $8 \times 7 = $ ___ $9 \times 7 = $ ___ $10 \times 7 = $ ___ $11 \times 7 = $ ___ $12 \times 7 = $ ___	$0 \times 7 = $ ___ $1 \times 7 = $ ___ $2 \times 7 = $ ___ $3 \times 7 = $ ___ $4 \times 7 = $ ___ $5 \times 7 = $ ___ $6 \times 7 = $ ___ $7 \times 7 = $ ___ $8 \times 7 = $ ___ $9 \times 7 = $ ___ $10 \times 7 = $ ___ $11 \times 7 = $ ___ $12 \times 7 = $ ___

Name _____ Date _____

ADDITION/MULTIPLICATION 9

DIRECTIONS: Find the sums and products.

1. $8 \times 0 = $ ___

2. $8 = $ ___ $= 8 \times 1 = $ ___

3. $8 + 8 = $ ___ $= 8 \times 2 = $ ___

4. $8 + 8 = $ ___ $+ 8 = $ ___ $= 8 \times 3 = $ ___

5. $8 + 8 = $ ___ $+ 8 = $ ___ $+ 8 = $ ___ $= 8 \times 4 = $ ___

6. $8 + 8 = $ ___ $+ 8 = $ ___ $+ 8 = $ ___ $+ 8 = $ ___ $= 8 \times 5 = $ ___

7. $8 + 8 = $ ___ $+ 8 = $ ___ $+ 8 = $ ___ $+ 8 = $ ___ $+ 8 = $ ___ $= 8 \times 6 = $ ___

8. $8 + 8 = $ ___ $+ 8 = $ ___ $+ 8 = $ ___ $+ 8 = $ ___ $+ 8 = $ ___ $+ 8 = $ ___ $= 8$

   $\times 7 = $ ___

9. $8 + 8 = $ ___ $+ 8 = $ ___ $+ 8 = $ ___ $+ 8 = $ ___ $+ 8 = $ ___ $+ 8 = $ ___ $+ 8$

   $= $ ___ $= 8 \times 8 = $ ___

10. $8 + 8 = $ ___ $+ 8 = $ ___ $+ 8$ ___ $+ 8 = $ ___ $+ 8 = $ ___ $+ 8 = $ ___ $+ 8 = $

   ___ $+ 8 = $ ___ $= 8 \times 9 = $ ___

11. $8 + 8 =$ ___ $+ 8 =$ ___ $+ 8 =$ ___ $+ 8 =$ ___ $+ 8 =$ ___ $+ 8 =$ ___ $+ 8$

$=$ ___ $+ 8 =$ ___ $+ 8 =$ ___ $= 8 \times 10 =$ ___

12. $8 + 8 =$ ___ $+ 8 =$ ___ $+ 8 =$ ___ $+ 8 =$ ___ $+ 8 =$ ___ $+ 8 =$

13. ___ $+ 8 =$ ___ $+ 8 =$ ___ $+ 8 =$ ___ $+ 8 =$ ___ $= 8 \times 11 =$ ___

14. $8 + 8 =$ ___ $+ 8 =$ ___ $+ 8 =$ ___ $+ 8 =$ ___ $+ 8 =$ ___ $+ 8 =$ ___ $+ 8$

$=$ ___ $+ 8 =$ ___ $+ 8 =$ ___ $+ 8 =$ ___ $+ 8 =$ ___ $= 8 \times 12 =$ ___

$0 \times 8 =$ ___ $1 \times 8 =$ ___ $2 \times 8 =$ ___ $3 \times 8 =$ ___ $4 \times 8 =$ ___ $5 \times 8 =$ ___ $6 \times 8 =$ ___ $7 \times 8 =$ ___ $8 \times 8 =$ ___ $9 \times 8 =$ ___ $10 \times 8 =$ ___ $11 \times 8 =$ ___ $12 \times 8 =$ ___		$0 \times 8 =$ ___ $1 \times 8 =$ ___ $2 \times 8 =$ ___ $3 \times 8 =$ ___ $4 \times 8 =$ ___ $5 \times 8 =$ ___ $6 \times 8 =$ ___ $7 \times 8 =$ ___ $8 \times 8 =$ ___ $9 \times 8 =$ ___ $10 \times 8 =$ ___ $11 \times 8 =$ ___ $12 \times 8 =$ ___	
$0 \times 8 =$ ___ $1 \times 8 =$ ___ $2 \times 8 =$ ___ $3 \times 8 =$ ___ $4 \times 8 =$ ___ $5 \times 8 =$ ___ $6 \times 8 =$ ___ $7 \times 8 =$ ___ $8 \times 8 =$ ___ $9 \times 8 =$ ___ $10 \times 8 =$ ___ $11 \times 8 =$ ___ $12 \times 8 =$ ___		$0 \times 8 =$ ___ $1 \times 8 =$ ___ $2 \times 8 =$ ___ $3 \times 8 =$ ___ $4 \times 8 =$ ___ $5 \times 8 =$ ___ $6 \times 8 =$ ___ $7 \times 8 =$ ___ $8 \times 8 =$ ___ $9 \times 8 =$ ___ $10 \times 8 =$ ___ $11 \times 8 =$ ___ $12 \times 8 =$ ___	

Name _____ Date _____

ADDITION/MULTIPLICATION 10

DIRECTIONS: Find the sums and products.

1. 9 x 0 = ___

2. 9 = ___ = 9 x 1 = ___

3. 9 + 9 = ___ = 9 x 2 = ___

4. 9 + 9 = ___ + 9 = ___ = 9 x 3 = ___

5. 9 + 9 = ___ + 9 = ___ + 9 = ___ = 9 x 4 = ___

6. 9 + 9 = ___ + 9 = ___ + 9 = ___ + 9 = ___ = 9 x 5 = ___

7. 9 + 9 = ___ + 9 = ___ + 9 = ___ + 9 = ___ + 9 = ___ = 9 x 6 =

    ___

8. 9 + 9 = ___ + 9 = ___ + 9 = ___ + 9 = ___ + 9 = ___ + 9 = ___

    = 9 x7 = ___

9. 9 + 9 = ___ + 9 = ___ + 9 = ___ + 9 = ___ + 9 = ___ + 9 = ___

    + 9 = ___ = 9 x 8 = ___

10. 9 + 9 = ___ + 9 = ___ + 9 ___ + 9 = ___ + 9 = ___ + 9 = ___ +

    9 = ___ + 9 = ___ = 9 x 9 = ___

11. $9 + 9 =$ ___ $+ 9 =$ ___ $+ 9 =$ ___ $+ 9 =$ ___ $+ 9 =$ ___ $+ 9 =$ ___

$+ 9 =$ ___ $+ 9 =$ ___ $+ 9 =$ ___ $= 9 \times 10 =$ ___

12. $9 + 9 =$ ___ $+ 9 =$ ___ $+ 9 =$ ___ $+ 9 =$ ___ $+ 9 =$ ___ $+ 9 =$ ___

$+ 9 =$ ___ $+ 9 =$ ___ $+ 9 =$ ___ $+ 9 =$ ___ $= 9 \times 11 =$ ___

13. $9 + 9 =$ ___ $+ 9 =$ ___ $+ 9 =$ ___ $+ 9 =$ ___ $+ 9 =$ ___ $+ 9 =$ ___

$+ 9 =$ ___ $+ 9 =$ ___ $+ 9 =$ ___ $+ 9 =$ ___ $+ 9 =$ ___ $= 9 \times 12 =$

___

$0 \times 9 =$ ___ $1 \times 9 =$ ___ $2 \times 9 =$ ___ $3 \times 9 =$ ___ $4 \times 9 =$ ___ $5 \times 9 =$ ___ $6 \times 9 =$ ___ $7 \times 9 =$ ___ $8 \times 9 =$ ___ $9 \times 9 =$ ___ $10 \times 9 =$ ___ $11 \times 9 =$ ___ $12 \times 9 =$ ___		$0 \times 9 =$ ___ $1 \times 9 =$ ___ $2 \times 9 =$ ___ $3 \times 9 =$ ___ $4 \times 9 =$ ___ $5 \times 9 =$ ___ $6 \times 9 =$ ___ $7 \times 9 =$ ___ $8 \times 9 =$ ___ $9 \times 9 =$ ___ $10 \times 9 =$ ___ $11 \times 9 =$ ___ $12 \times 9 =$ ___	
$0 \times 9 =$ ___ $1 \times 9 =$ ___ $2 \times 9 =$ ___ $3 \times 9 =$ ___ $4 \times 9 =$ ___ $5 \times 9 =$ ___ $6 \times 9 =$ ___ $7 \times 9 =$ ___ $8 \times 9 =$ ___ $9 \times 9 =$ ___ $10 \times 9 =$ ___ $11 \times 9 =$ ___ $12 \times 9 =$ ___		$0 \times 9 =$ ___ $1 \times 9 =$ ___ $2 \times 9 =$ ___ $3 \times 9 =$ ___ $4 \times 9 =$ ___ $5 \times 9 =$ ___ $6 \times 9 =$ ___ $7 \times 9 =$ ___ $8 \times 9 =$ ___ $9 \times 9 =$ ___ $10 \times 9 =$ ___ $11 \times 9 =$ ___ $12 \times 9 =$ ___	

Name _____ Date _____

ADDITION/MULTIPLICATION 11

DIRECTIONS: Find the sums and products.

1. $10 \times 0 = $ ___

2. $10 = $ ___ $ = 10 \times 1 = $ ___

3. $10 + 10 = $ ___ $ = 10 \times 2 = $ ___

4. $10 + 10 = $ ___ $ + 10 = $ ___ $ = 10 \times 3 = $ ___

5. $10 + 10 = $ ___ $ + 10 = $ ___ $ + 10 = $ ___ $ = 10 \times 4 = $ ___

6. $10 + 10 = $ ___ $ + 10 = $ ___ $ + 10 = $ ___ $ + 10 = $ ___ $ = 10 \times 5 = $ ___

7. $10 + 10 = $ ___ $ + 10 = $ ___ $ + 10 = $ ___ $ + 10 = $ ___ $ + 10 = $ ___ $ = 10 \times$

    $6 = $ ___

8. $10 + 10 = $ ___ $ + 10 = $ ___ $ + 10 = $ ___ $ + 10 = $ ___ $ + 10 = $ ___ $ + 10$

    $ = $ ___ $ = 10 \times 7 = $ ___

9. $10 + 10 = $ ___ $ + 10 = $ ___ $ + 10 = $ ___ $ + 10 = $ ___ $ + 10 = $ ___ $ + 10$

    $ = $ ___ $ + 10 = $ ___ $ = 10 \times 8 = $ ___

10. $10 + 10 = $ ___ $ + 10 = $ ___ $ + 10$ ___ $ + 10 = $ ___ $ + 10 = $ ___ $ + 10 = $

    ___ $ + 10 = $ ___ $ + 10 = $ ___ $ = 10 \times 9 = $ ___

11. $10 + 10 =$ ___ $+ 10 =$ ___ $+ 10 =$ ___ $+ 10 =$ ___ $+ 10 =$ ___ $+ 10$

= ___ $+ 10 =$ ___ $+ 10 =$ ___ $+ 10 =$ ___ $= 10 \times 10 =$ ___

12. $10 + 10 =$ ___ $+ 10 =$ ___ $+ 10 =$ ___ $+ 10 =$ ___ $+ 10 =$ ___ $+ 10$

= ___ $+ 10 =$ ___ $+ 10 =$ ___ $+ 10 =$ ___ $= 10 \times 11 =$

___

13. $10 + 10 =$ ___ $+ 10 =$ ___ $+ 10 =$ ___ $+ 10 =$ ___ $+ 10 =$ ___ $+ 10$

= ___ $+ 10 =$ ___ $+ 10 =$ ___ $+ 10 =$ ___ $+ 10 =$ ___ $=$

$10 \times 12 =$ ___

$0 \times 10 =$ ___ $1 \times 10 =$ ___ $2 \times 10 =$ ___ $3 \times 10 =$ ___ $4 \times 10 =$ ___ $5 \times 10 =$ ___ $6 \times 10 =$ ___ $7 \times 10 =$ ___ $8 \times 10 =$ ___ $9 \times 10 =$ ___ $10 \times 10 =$ ___ $11 \times 10 =$ ___ $12 \times 10 =$ ___	$0 \times 10 =$ ___ $1 \times 10 =$ ___ $2 \times 10 =$ ___ $3 \times 10 =$ ___ $4 \times 10 =$ ___ $5 \times 10 =$ ___ $6 \times 10 =$ ___ $7 \times 10 =$ ___ $8 \times 10 =$ ___ $9 \times 10 =$ ___ $10 \times 10 =$ ___ $11 \times 10 =$ ___ $12 \times 10 =$ ___
$0 \times 10 =$ ___ $1 \times 10 =$ ___ $2 \times 10 =$ ___ $3 \times 10 =$ ___ $4 \times 10 =$ ___ $5 \times 10 =$ ___ $6 \times 10 =$ ___ $7 \times 10 =$ ___ $8 \times 10 =$ ___ $9 \times 10 =$ ___ $10 \times 10 =$ ___ $11 \times 10 =$ ___ $12 \times 10 =$ ___	$0 \times 10 =$ ___ $1 \times 10 =$ ___ $2 \times 10 =$ ___ $3 \times 10 =$ ___ $4 \times 10 =$ ___ $5 \times 10 =$ ___ $6 \times 10 =$ ___ $7 \times 10 =$ ___ $8 \times 10 =$ ___ $9 \times 10 =$ ___ $10 \times 10 =$ ___ $11 \times 10 =$ ___ $12 \times 10 =$ ___

Nettie Whitney Bailey

Name _____ Date _____

ADDITION/MULTIPLICATION 12

DIRECTIONS: Find the sums and products.

1. 11 x 0 = ___

2. 11 = ___ = 11 x 1 = ___

3. 11 + 11 = ___ = 11 x 2 = ___

4. 11 + 11 = ___ + 11 = ___ = 11 x 3 = ___

5. 11 + 11 = ___ + 11 = ___ + 11 = ___ = 11 x 4 = ___

6. 11 + 11 = ___ + 11= ___ + 11 = ___ + 11 = ___ = 11 x 5 = ___

7. 11 + 11 = ___ + 11 = ___ + 11 = ___ + 11 = ___ + 11 = ___ = 11 x

    6 = ___

8. 11 + 11 = ___ + 11 = ___ + 11 = ___ + 11 = ___ + 11 = ___ + 11

    = ___ = 11 x 7 = ___

9. 11 + 11 = ___ + 11 = ___ + 11 = ___ + 11 = ___ + 11 = ___ + 11

    = ___ + 11 = ___ = 11 x 8 = ___

10. 11 + 11 = ___ + 11 = ___ + 11 ___ + 11 = ___ + 11 = ___ + 11 =

    ___ + 11 = ___ + 11 = ___ = 11 x 9 = ___

11. $11 + 11 = \underline{\quad} + 11 = \underline{\quad} + 11 = \underline{\quad} + 11 = \underline{\quad} + 11 = \underline{\quad} + 11$

$= \underline{\quad} + 11 = \underline{\quad} + 11 = \underline{\quad} + 11 = \underline{\quad} = 11 \times 10 = \underline{\quad}$

12. $11 + 11 = \underline{\quad} + 11 = \underline{\quad} + 11 = \underline{\quad} + 11 = \underline{\quad} + 11 = \underline{\quad} + 11$

$= \underline{\quad} + 11 = \underline{\quad} + 11 = \underline{\quad} + 11 = \underline{\quad} + 11 = \underline{\quad} = 11 \times 11 =$

$\underline{\quad}$

13. $11 + 11 = \underline{\quad} + 11 = \underline{\quad} + 11 = \underline{\quad} + 11 = \underline{\quad} + 11 = \underline{\quad} + 11$

$= \underline{\quad} + 11 = \underline{\quad} + 11 = \underline{\quad} + 11 = \underline{\quad} + 11 = \underline{\quad} + 11 = \underline{\quad} =$

$11 \times 12 = \underline{\quad}$

$0 \times 11 = \underline{\quad}$ $1 \times 11 = \underline{\quad}$ $2 \times 11 = \underline{\quad}$ $3 \times 11 = \underline{\quad}$ $4 \times 11 = \underline{\quad}$ $5 \times 11 = \underline{\quad}$ $6 \times 11 = \underline{\quad}$ $7 \times 11 = \underline{\quad}$ $8 \times 11 = \underline{\quad}$ $9 \times 11 = \underline{\quad}$ $10 \times 11 = \underline{\quad}$ $11 \times 11 = \underline{\quad}$ $12 \times 11 = \underline{\quad}$	$0 \times 11 = \underline{\quad}$ $1 \times 11 = \underline{\quad}$ $2 \times 11 = \underline{\quad}$ $3 \times 11 = \underline{\quad}$ $4 \times 11 = \underline{\quad}$ $5 \times 11 = \underline{\quad}$ $6 \times 11 = \underline{\quad}$ $7 \times 11 = \underline{\quad}$ $8 \times 11 = \underline{\quad}$ $9 \times 11 = \underline{\quad}$ $10 \times 11 = \underline{\quad}$ $11 \times 11 = \underline{\quad}$ $12 \times 11 = \underline{\quad}$
$0 \times 11 = \underline{\quad}$ $1 \times 11 = \underline{\quad}$ $2 \times 11 = \underline{\quad}$ $3 \times 11 = \underline{\quad}$ $4 \times 11 = \underline{\quad}$ $5 \times 11 = \underline{\quad}$ $6 \times 11 = \underline{\quad}$ $7 \times 11 = \underline{\quad}$ $8 \times 11 = \underline{\quad}$ $9 \times 11 = \underline{\quad}$ $10 \times 11 = \underline{\quad}$ $11 \times 11 = \underline{\quad}$ $12 \times 11 = \underline{\quad}$	$0 \times 11 = \underline{\quad}$ $1 \times 11 = \underline{\quad}$ $2 \times 11 = \underline{\quad}$ $3 \times 11 = \underline{\quad}$ $4 \times 11 = \underline{\quad}$ $5 \times 11 = \underline{\quad}$ $6 \times 11 = \underline{\quad}$ $7 \times 11 = \underline{\quad}$ $8 \times 11 = \underline{\quad}$ $9 \times 11 = \underline{\quad}$ $10 \times 11 = \underline{\quad}$ $11 \times 11 = \underline{\quad}$ $12 \times 11 = \underline{\quad}$

Name _____ Date _____

ADDITION/MULTIPLICATION 13

DIRECTIONS: Find the sums and products.

1. $12 \times 0 =$ ___

2. $12 =$ ___ $= 12 \times 1 =$ ___

3. $12 + 12 =$ ___ $= 12 \times 2 =$ ___

4. $12 + 12 =$ ___ $+ 12 =$ ___ $= 12 \times 3 =$ ___

5. $12 + 12 =$ ___ $+ 12 =$ ___ $+ 12 =$ ___ $= 12 \times 4 =$ ___

6. $12 =$ ___ $+ 12 =$ ___ $+ 12 =$ ___ $+ 12 =$ ___ $+ 12 =$ ___ $= 12 \times 5 =$

   ___

7. $12 + 12 =$ ___ $+ 12 =$ ___ $+ 12 =$ ___ $+ 12 =$ ___ $+ 12 =$ ___ $= 12 \times$

   $6 =$ ___

8. $12 + 12 =$ ___ $+ 12 =$ ___ $+ 12 =$ ___ $+ 12 =$ ___ $+ 12 =$ ___ $+ 12$

   $=$ ___ $= 12 \times 7 =$ ___

9. $12 + 12 =$ ___ $+ 12 =$ ___ $+ 12 =$ ___ $+ 12 =$ ___ $+ 12 =$ ___ $+ 12$

   $=$ ___ $+ 12 =$ ___ $= 12 \times 8 =$ ___

10.   12 + 12 = ___ + 12 = ___ + 12 ___ + 12 = ___ + 12 = ___ + 12 =

___ + 12 = ___ + 12 = ___ = 12 x 9 = ___

11.   12 + 12 = ___ + 12 = ___ + 12 = ___ + 12 = ___ + 12 = ___ + 12

= ___ + 12 = ___ + 12 = ___ + 12 = ___ = 12 x 10 = ___

12.   12 + 12 = ___ + 12 = ___ + 12 = ___ + 12 = ___ + 12 = ___ + 12

= ___ +12 = ___ + 12 = ___ + 12 = ___ + = ___ = 12 x 11 = ___

13.   12 + 12 = ___ + 12 = ___ + 12 = ___ + 12 = ___ + 12 = ___ + 12

= ___ + 12 = ___ + 12 = ___ + 12 = ___ + 12 = ___ + 12 = ___ =

12 x 12 = ___

0 x 12 = ___ 1 x 12 = ___ 2 x 12 = ___ 3 x 12 = ___ 4 x 12 = ___ 5 x 12 = ___ 6 x 12 = ___ 7 x 12 = ___ 8 x 12 = ___ 9 x 12 = ___ 10 x 12 = ___ 11 x 12 = ___ 12 x 12 = ___	0 x 12 = ___ 1 x 12 = ___ 2 x 12 = ___ 3 x 12 = ___ 4 x 12 = ___ 5 x 12 = ___ 6 x 12 = ___ 7 x 12 = ___ 8 x 12 = ___ 9 x 12 = ___ 10 x 12 = ___ 11 x 12 = ___ 12 x 12 = ___
0 x 12 = ___ 1 x 12 = ___ 2 x 12 = ___ 3 x 12 = ___ 4 x 12 = ___ 5 x 12 = ___ 6 x 12 = ___ 7 x 12 = ___ 8 x 12 = ___ 9 x 12 = ___ 10 x 12 = ___ 11 x 12 = ___ 12 x 12 = ___	0 x 12 = ___ 1 x 12 = ___ 2 x 12 = ___ 3 x 12 = ___ 4 x 12 = ___ 5 x 12 = ___ 6 x 12 = ___ 7 x 12 = ___ 8 x 12 = ___ 9 x 12 = ___ 10 x 12 = ___ 11 x 12 = ___ 12 x 12 = ___

Nettie Whitney Bailey

MULTIPLICATION TABLE

Give the MULTIPLICATION TABLE to each student that does not KNOW his/her times tables, still counting on fingers, drawing circles or sticks, or saying products in order to figure out answers. Teach them how to use it and direct them to use it when solving multiplication and division problems. This will enable them to get correct answers as well as learn the multiplication facts.

Name _____

MULTIPLICATION TABLE

X	0	1	2	3	4	5	6	7	8	9	10	11	12
0	0	0	0	0	0	0	0	0	0	0	0	0	0
1	0	1	2	3	4	5	6	7	8	9	10	11	12
2	0	2	4	6	8	10	12	14	16	18	20	22	24
3	0	3	6	9	12	15	18	21	24	27	30	33	36
4	0	4	8	12	16	20	24	28	32	36	40	44	48
5	0	5	10	15	20	25	30	35	40	45	50	55	60
6	0	6	12	18	24	30	36	42	48	54	60	66	72
7	0	7	14	21	28	35	42	49	56	63	70	77	84
8	0	8	16	24	32	40	48	56	64	72	80	88	96
9	0	9	18	27	36	45	54	63	72	81	90	99	108
10	0	10	20	30	40	50	60	70	80	90	100	110	120
11	0	11	22	33	44	55	66	77	88	99	110	121	132
12	0	12	24	36	48	60	72	84	96	108	120	132	144

Name _____ Date _____

DIVISION 1

DIRECTIONS: Solve. Remember your times tables.

Think: If 5 x 9 = 45, then 45 ÷ 9 = 5 and 45 ÷ 5 = 9.

1. 48 ÷ 6 =	12 ÷ 6 =	9 ÷ 0 =	28 ÷ 7 =	81 ÷ 9 =	72 ÷ 9=
2. 6 ÷ 0 =	36 ÷ 6 =	99 ÷ 11 =	10 ÷ 5 =	49 ÷ 7 =	66 ÷ 6=
3. 14 ÷ 2 =	48 ÷ 8 =	18 ÷ 3 =	27 ÷ 9 =	80 ÷ 8 =	9 ÷3=
4. 6 ÷ 2 =	15 ÷ 5 =	12 ÷ 2 =	8 ÷ 0 =	32 ÷ 8 =	44 ÷ 11 =
5. 20 ÷ 4 =	16 ÷ 2 =	60 ÷ 5 =	50 ÷ 10 =	22 ÷ 2 =	35 ÷ 5 =
6. 42 ÷ 7 =	56 ÷ 8 =	18 ÷ 2 =	72 ÷ 8 =	66 ÷ 11 =	15 ÷ 3 =
7. 30 ÷ 10 =	45 ÷ 9 =	70 ÷ 7 =	10 ÷ 2 =	44 ÷ 4 =	20 ÷ 5 =
8. 40 ÷ 5 =	77 ÷ 11 =	90 ÷ 10 =	70 ÷ 10 =	18 ÷ 6 =	4 ÷ 2 =
9. 7 ÷ 0 =	35 ÷ 5 =	64 ÷ 8 =	42 ÷ 6 =	22 ÷ 11 =	30 ÷ 3 =
10. 18 ÷ 9 =	40 ÷ 8 =	45 ÷ 5 =	56 ÷ 7 =	77 ÷ 7 =	50 ÷ 5 =
11. 50 ÷ 5 =	16 ÷ 4 =	25 ÷ 5 =	8 ÷ 2 =	63 ÷9 =	100 ÷ 10 =
12. 14 ÷ 7 =	6 ÷ 3 =	90 ÷ 10 =	60 ÷ 12 =	28 ÷ 4 =	63 ÷ 7 =

Name _____ Date _____

DIVISION 2

DIRECTIONS: Study the example. Answer the questions. Rewrite the problem in the usual form. Solve and check the problems.

Example: $84 \div 2 = 42$ $\qquad$ $42 \times 2 = 84$

1. Which numeral is the divisor?_____ The dividend?_____ The quotient?_____

2. What are the steps that must be taken to solve a division problem?

1. _____
2. _____
3. _____
4. _____
5. _____
6. _____
7. _____
8. _____

3. How do you check a division problem? Multiply the_____ by the _____. If your problem is right, that (product) answer will be the same as the dividend.

4. $68 \div 2 =$ $\quad$ $96 \div 3 =$ $\quad$ $42 \div 2 =$ $\quad$ $84 \div 2 =$ $\quad$ $60 \div 3 =$

5. $55 \div 1 =$ $\quad$ $30 \div 3 =$ $\quad$ $60 \div 6 =$ $\quad$ $92 \div 1 =$ $\quad$ $26 \div 2 =$

6. $284 \div 4 =$ $\quad$ $426 \div 6 =$ $\quad$ $189 \div 3 =$ $\quad$ $366 \div 6 =$ $\quad$ $320 \div 8 =$

Name _____ Date _____

DIVISION 3

DIRECTIONS: Study the example. Answer the questions. Solve and check the problems.

Example: $213 \div 3 =$ 71 71 x 3 = 213

1. Which numeral is the divisor?_____ The dividend?_____ The quotient?_____

2. What are the steps that must be taken to solve a division problem?

     1. _____
     2. _____
     3. _____
     4. _____
     5. _____
     6. _____
     7. _____
     8. _____

3. How do you check a division problem? Multiply the_____ by the _____ and add the _____ if there is one. If your problem is right, that sum (answer) will be the same as the dividend.

4. $148 \div 2 =$ $100 \div 2 =$ $728 \div 8 =$ $427 \div 7 =$ $205 \div 5 =$

5. $155 \div 3 =$ $369 \div 4 =$ $246 \div 8 =$ $187 \div 2 =$ $482 \div 8 =$

6. $326 \div 4 =$ $251 \div 5 =$ $814 \div 9 =$ $359 \div 7 =$ $278 \div 9 =$

Name _____ Date _____

DIVISION 4

DIRECTIONS: Study the example. Answer the questions. Solve and check the problems.

Example: $240 \div 5 = 48$ $\qquad$ $48 \times 5 = 240$

1. Which numeral is the divisor?_____ The dividend?_____ The quotient?_____

2. What are the steps that must be taken to solve a division problem?

1. _____	7. _____
2. _____	8. _____
3. _____	9. _____
4. _____	10. _____
5. _____	11. _____
6. _____	12. _____

3. How do you check a division problem? Multiply the _____ by the _____ and add the _____ if there is one. If your problem is right, that sum (answer) will be the same as the dividend.

4. $684 \div 6 =$ $\quad$ $847 \div 7 =$ $\quad$ $888 \div 8 =$ $\quad$ $936 \div 9 =$ $\quad$ $640 \div 6 =$

5. $324 \div 3 =$ $\quad$ $456 \div 2 =$ $\quad$ $744 \div 6 =$ $\quad$ $924 \div 7 =$ $\quad$ $981 \div 9 =$

6. $154 \div 5 =$ $\quad$ $125 \div 4 =$ $\quad$ $129 \div 2 =$ $\quad$ $120 \div 3 =$ $\quad$ $542 \div 6 =$

Name _____ Date _____

DIVISION 5

DIRECTIONS: Study the example. Answer the questions. Solve and check the problems.

Example: $644 \div 8 = 80$ r.4 $80 \times 8 = 640 + 4 = 644$

1 . Which numeral is the divisor?_____ The dividend?_____ The quotient?_____ The remainder? ____

2. What are the steps that must be taken to solve a division problem?

1. _____   7. _____
2. _____   8. _____
3. _____   9. _____
4. _____   10. _____
5. _____   11. _____
6. _____   12. _____

3. How do you check a division problem? Multiply the _____ by the _____ and add the _____ if there is one. If your problem is right, that sum (answer) will be the same as the dividend.

4. $275 \div 3 =$ $201 \div 4 =$ $567 \div 4 =$ $302 \div 6 =$ $246 \div 4 =$

5. $306 \div 5 =$ $165 \div 8 =$ $352 \div 5 =$ $169 \div 4 =$ $641 \div 8 =$

6. $633 \div 9 =$ $402 \div 8 =$ $218 \div 3 =$ $453 \div 5 =$ $490 \div 7 =$

Name _____ Date _____

ODD NUMBERS

DIRECTIONS: Complete this table with odd numerals.

1		5		9		13			19
	23		27		31			37	
				49			55		
61						73			
		85							99
101					111				119
			127				135		
	143			149				157	
161						173			
									199

Name _____ Date _____

EVEN NUMBERS

DIRECTIONS: Put an X on all the boxes that contain even numerals.

1	2	3	4	5	6	7	8	9	10
11	12	13	14	15	16	17	18	19	20
21	22	23	24	25	26	27	28	29	30
31	32	33	34	35	36	37	38	39	40
41	42	43	44	45	46	47	48	49	50
51	52	53	54	55	56	57	58	59	60
61	62	63	64	65	66	67	68	69	70
71	72	73	74	75	76	77	78	79	80
81	82	83	84	85	86	87	88	89	90
91	92	93	94	95	96	97	98	99	100
101	102	103	104	105	106	107	108	109	110
111	112	113	114	115	116	117	118	119	120
121	122	123	124	125	126	127	128	129	130
131	132	133	134	135	136	137	138	139	140
141	142	143	144	145	146	147	148	149	150
151	152	153	154	155	156	157	158	159	160
161	162	163	164	165	166	167	168	169	170
171	172	173	174	175	176	177	178	179	180
181	182	183	184	185	186	187	188	189	190
191	192	193	194	195	196	197	198	199	200

Name _____ Date _____

NUMBER SENTENCES 1

DIRECTIONS: Write the sums and differences. Circle the number sentence if it is true.

Example: $6 + 6 = 8 + 9$ $6 + 6 = 8 + 4$

(12 = 17)   (12 = 12)

(1)

$11 + 7 = 3 + 8$

$11 + 7 = 4 + 3$

$11 + 7 = 1 + 7$

$11 + 7 = 7 + 11$

(2)

$5 + 10 = 8 + 1$

$5 + 10 = 9 + 6$

$5 + 10 = 1 + 10$

$5 + 10 = 5 + 5$

(3)

$12 + 8 = 8 + 2$

$12 + 8 = 4 + 9$

$12 + 8 = 20 - 0$

$12 + 8 = 11 + 8$

(4)

$17 - 10 = 9 + 8$

$17 - 10 = 5 + 2$

$17 - 10 = 10 + 7$

$17 - 10 = 17 - 0$

(5)

$25 - 24 = 25 + 24$

$25 - 24 = 15 + 14$

$25 - 24 = 15 - 14$

$25 - 24 = 14 + 25$

(6)

$33 + 10 = 10 + 23$

$33 + 10 = 33 - 10$

$33 + 10 = 20 + 23$

$33 + 10 = 15 + 18$

Name _____

(7)	**(8)**	**(9)**
$13 - 9 = 4 + 5$	$16 - 8 = 8 + 4$	$18 - 8 = 10 + 8$
$13 - 9 = 9 + 13$	$16 - 8 = 9 + 7$	$18 - 8 = 8 + 2$
$13 - 9 = 0 + 4$	$16 - 8 = 16 + 0$	$18 - 8 = 8 + 10$
$13 - 9 = 7 + 6$	$16 - 8 = 10 - 2$	$18 - 8 = 9 + 9$

(10)

$24 + 15 = 24 - 15$

$24 + 15 = 20 + 19$

$24 + 15 = 19 + 15$

$24 + 15 = 39 + 15$

DIRECTIONS: Write the sums and differences. Circle the number sentences that are NOT true.

(11)	**(12)**
$17 + 17 = 34 + 0$	$66 - 26 = 0 + 40$
$17 + 17 = 44 - 10$	$66 - 26 = 20 + 20$
$17 + 17 = 17 - 17$	$66 - 26 = 6 + 34$
$17 + 17 = 19 + 15$	$66 - 26 = 66 + 26$

Name _____ Date _____

NUMBER SENTENCES 2

DIRECTIONS: Find the numeral that belongs in each box to make the number sentences true.

Examples: $7 + 6 = 7 +$ $(\square + 2)\ 7 + 6 = 7 + (4 + 2)$

$7 = 7\ 6 = ? + 2\ 7 = 7$ $6 = 4 + 2$

(1)

a. $10 + 7 = (\square + 8) + 7$

b. $8 + 6 = 8 + (3 + \square)$

c. $15 + 7 = (\square + 11) + 7$

d. $6 + 12 = 6 + (5 + \square)$

(2)

a. $4 + 10 = 4 + (\square + 5)$

b. $8 + 13 = (\square + 7) + 13$

c. $1 + 3 = 1 + (1 + \square)$

d. $12 - 9 = (\square + 6) - 9$

(3)

a. $15 - 8 = (\square + 0) - 8$

b. $11 + 3 = 11 + (2 + \square)$

c. $16 - 10 = (\square + 4) - 10$

d. $7 - 2 = 7 - (2 + \square)$

(4)

a. $3 + 9 = 3 + (\square + 7)$

b. $19 - 3 = (\square + 9) + 3$

c. $9 + 2 = 9 + (0 + \square)$

d. $12 - 2 = (\square + 3) - 2$

(5)

a. $13 + 25 = (\square + 1) + 25$

(6)

a. $18 + 19 = 18 + (\square + 12)$

Nettie Whitney Bailey

Name _____

b. $17 + 15 = 17 + (3 \times \square)$ b. $17 - 8 = (\square + 4) - 8$

c. $14 - 14 = (\square \times 2) - 14$ c. $22 + 15 = 22 + (3 \times \square)$

d. $12 + 16 = 12 + (4 \times \square)$ d. $36 - 11 = (\square \times 6) - 11$

(7)

a. $32 + 10 = (2 \times \square) + 10$

b. $23 - 8 = 23 - (8 \times \square)$

c. $19 - 12 = (0 \times \square) - 12$

d. $15 + 18 = (\square \times 5) + (3 \times \square)$

DIRECTION: Circle the number sentences that are NOT true.

(8)

a. $16 + 13 = (4 \times 4) + (13 \times 0)$

b. $50 + 35 = (5 \times 10) + (5 \times 7)$

c. $39 \times 13 = (13 \times 3) \times (1 \times 13)$

d. $72 \times 132 = (9 \times 8) \times (11 \times 11)$

(9)

a. $20 + 17 = (2 \times 10) + (34 - 17)$

b. $33 + 0 = (11 \times 3) + (0 \times 1)$

c. $52 - 48 = (9 \times 6) - 4 \times 12$

d. $144 - 100 = (12 \times 12) - (10 \times 10)$

166

Name _____ Date _____

PLACE VALUE 1
NUMBER SENSE

DIRECTION: Write the numerals in the chart.

1) 12	**2)** 16,057	**3)** 9	**4)** 246,680
5) 1,305	**6)** 100	**7)** 272	**8)** 40
	9) 505		**10)** 3,708

	H Th	T Th	Th	H	T	O
1						
2						
3						
4						
5						
6						
7						
8						
9						
10						

DIRECTION: Write the numerals.

11. one hundred _____

Name _____

12. three hundred fifty _____
13. nine hundred twenty _____
14. eight hundred four _____
15. two thousand _____
16. nine thousand, three hundred _____
17. four thousand, five hundred _____
18. six thousand, six hundred sixty_____
19. ten thousand, seven hundred four _____

DIRECTION: Circle the odd numerals.

25   38   66   17   40   99   3

DIRECTION: Circle the even numerals.

94   66   71   4   50   33   22

DIRECTION: Write these numerals in order from the least to the greatest.

205   793   764   109   32,601   243
850   829   1,629,   905

_____, _____, _____, _____, _____,

_____, _____, _____, _____,_____

Name _____   Date _____

PLACE VALUE 2

	100 TRL	10 TRL	TRL	100 BIL	10 BIL	B	100 MIL	10 MIL	MIL	100 TH	10 TH	TH	H	T	O
A	1	0	0	0	0	0	0	0	0	0	0	0	0	0	0
B		4	5	0	7	3	0	0	6	1	9	0	3	3	3
C			2	9	0	0	7	7	3	4	0	0	4	0	5
D				3	6	2	0	9	0	6	8	0	1	0	0
E					7	0	8	0	5	0	1	0	0	9	0
F						5	1	4	6	9	3	2	8	7	0
G							9	0	3	0	1	0	6	0	9
H								8	5	0	5	1	0	1	0
I									1	1	0	2	3	0	6
J										5	0	0	0	0	0
K											2	5	6	0	4
L												3	9	9	0
M													4	1	0

169

Name _____ Date _____

PLACE VALUE 2

DIRECTIONS: Write the name of each numeral on the chart in words. Use the column headings to help you.

A. _____

B. _____

C. _____

D. _____

E. _____

F. _____

G. _____

H. _____

I _____

J. _____

K. _____

L. _____

M. _____

DIRECTION: Write the numerals for the following number names.

1. Three hundred forty-four thousand, six hundred seventy-eight

_____

2. Four million, three hundred fifty thousand_____

3. One billion, nine hundred nine million, one hundred ten thousand, two hundred eighty_____

Name _____ Date _____

SUBTRACTING WITH REGROUPING (ZEROES) I

DIRECTIONS: Solve. Check your work by adding the subtrahend (bottom number) and the difference (answer). Your answer (sum) is correct if it is the same as the minuend (top number).

Example: 50 - 25 = 25 Check: 25 + 25 = 50

1.
10	80	30	60	90	70	50	20
8	2	7	6	5	4	1	3

2.
20	90	40	70	60	30	50	80
15	54	36	43	32	29	41	68

Nettie Whitney Bailey

Name _____ Date _____

SUBTRACTING WITH REGROUPING (ZEROES) II

DIRECTIONS: Solve. Check your work by adding the subtrahend (bottom number) and the difference (answer). Your answer (sum) is correct if it is the same as the minuend (top number).

Example: 490 - 246 = 244 Check: 246 + 244 = 490

1. 120	390	580	850	730
12	41	134	615	727
2. 660	980	250	740	470
139	268	111	333	206
3. 930	660	810	540	470
32	51	615	399	184
4. 201	709	307	801	404
59	515	135	222	185
5. 700	200	100	500	600
401	34	67	92	45
6. 800	900	400	300	100
323	316	179	151	5

Name _____ Date _____

SUBTRACTING WITH REGROUPING (ZEROES) III

DIRECTIONS: Solve. Check your work by adding the subtrahend (bottom number) and the difference (answer). Your answer (sum) is correct if it is the same as the minuend (top number).

Example: 5,005 - 2,345 = 2,660 Check: 2,345 + 2,660 = 5,005

1. 7,530	2,340	8,090	4,050	6,006
2,617	1.456	3,645	1,999	1,236
2. 1,008	5,009	9,007	3,000	7,003
356	799	3,478	2,050	1,007
3. 2,000	5,000	3,000	6,000	9,000
50	346	1,270	2,809	3,012
4. 8.000	5,000	4,000	7,000	2,000
2,468	3,133	2,799	6.995	1,462

Nettie Whitney Bailey

Name _____ Date _____

SUBTRACTING WITH REGROUPING (ZEROES) IV

DIRECTIONS: Solve. Check your work by adding the subtrahend (bottom number) and the difference (answer). Your answer (sum) is correct if it is the same as the minuend (top number).

Example: 20,058 - 11,969 = 8,089 Check: 11,969 + 8,089 = 20,058

1. 55,440	90,304	81,065	77,002
23,976	77,153	14,629	34,567
2. 65,900	30,003	40,078	20,007
20,850	9,870	15,567	4,329
3. 350,986	906,306	777,000	400,444
131,097	550,039	257,752	196,555
4. 500,906	620,001	800,008	300,003
111.810	306,019	700,067	100,004

Name _____ Date _____

SUBTRACTING WITH REGROUPING (ZEROES) V

Review

DIRECTIONS: Solve and check.

1.
90	500	300	700	2,000
6	2	25	241	75

2.
5,000	9,000	11,000	50,000
675	2,323	8	11

3.
45,000	73,000	26,000	790,000
429	1,357	16,798	6

4.
540,000	630,000	820,000	230,000
43	632	7,489	15,555

5.
460,000	400,000	700,000	600,000
1,678	61,102	636,099	434,082

FRACTION PRACTICE

Fraction Practice can be used as a pretest or as a post test to assess the students' knowledge of fractions.

Name _____ Date _____

FRACTION PRACTICE

DIRECTION: Answer the questions with complete sentences.

1. What is a fraction? _____

_____

2. Describe a proper fraction? _____

_____

3. Write 5 proper fractions. _____

_____

4. Describe an improper fraction? _____

_____

5. Write 5 improper fractions. _____

_____

6. What is a mixed number? _____

_____

7. Write 5 mixed numbers. _____

_____

8. What does equivalent mean? (Circle the correct answers.)
   A. less than   B. equal to   C. greater than   D. the same as

9. Write 3 fractions that are equivalent to 1/4: _____

_____

10. Describe how you changed the fraction. _____

_____

11. Reduce or simplify this fraction: 6/8 _____

_____

12. Describe how you changed the fraction. _____

_____

13. Change these mixed numbers to improper fractions:
   $2 \frac{3}{8}$ = _____ $7 \frac{4}{5}$ = _____ $6 \frac{7}{8}$ = _____ $10 \frac{1}{2}$ = _____ $1 \frac{3}{4}$ = _____

14. Describe how you changed the mixed numbers. _____

_____

15. Change the improper fractions you wrote for #5 to mixed numbers.

_____

16. Describe how you changed the improper fractions.

_____

NAMES OF FRACTIONS

This can be used as part of the Mathematics bulletin board and/or each student can have a copy for reference.

Name _____ Date _____

NAMES OF FRACTIONS

When you say the name of a fraction, say the name of the top number, which is called the numerator, and then say the name of the bottom number, which is called the denominator, adding "th" or "ths" to its name.

> *Example:* 2/4 = two-fourths; 1/5 = one-fifth; 3/6 = three-sixths
> 1/7 = one-seventh; etc.

There are two exceptions to this rule.

When "2" is the denominator, it is read half or halves.
Examples: ½ = one-half; $^{6}/_{2}$ = six-halves

When "3" is the denominator, it is read third or thirds.
Examples: 1/3 = one-third; 2/3 = two-thirds

When there is a whole number and a fraction, it is called a mixed number. Say the whole number, say the word "and", then say the name of the fraction.
Examples: 5 ¾ = five and three-fourths; 10 $^{2}/_{7}$ = ten and two-sevenths

Name _____ Date _____

WRITING THE NAMES OF FRACTIONS

DIRECTION: Write the names of the fractions and mixed numbers.

1. 3/4 _____

2. 7/8 _____

3. 15/6 _____

4. 7 8/9 _____

5. 12/17 _____

6. 35 1/2 _____

7. 2/13 _____

8. 1/2 _____

9. 2/3 _____

10. 50/25 _____

Name _____ Date _____

WRITING EQUIVALENT FRACTIONS BY MULTIPLYING 1

DIRECTION: Write equivalent fractions by multiplying the numerators and denominators by the numbers in parentheses.

1. (2) 1/2=   8/9=   2/3=   4/5=   6/7=

2. (3) 1/4=   3/11=   5/6=   1/4=   2/9=

3. (4) 4/7=   2/9=   3/7=   1/3=   7/9=

4. (5) 3/5=   5/7=   1/8=   4/11=   1/6=

5. (6) 4/9=   1/2=   8/9=   2/3=   4/5=

Nettie Whitney Bailey

Name _____ Date _____

WRITING EQUIVALENT FRACTIONS BY MULTIPLYING 2

DIRECTION: Write equivalent fractions by multiplying the numerators and denominators by the numbers in parentheses.

1. (2) 6/7=   3/4=   3/11=   5/6=   1/4=

2. (4) 2/9=   4/7=   2/9=   3/7=   1/3=

3. (6) 7/9=   3/5=   5/7=   1/8=   4/11=

4. (3) 1/6=   4/9=   1/2=   8/9=   2/3=

5. (5) 4/5=   6/7=   3/4=   3/11=   5/6=

6. (7) 4/7=   2/9=   3/7=   1/3=   7/9=

7. (9) 4/9=   5/7=   1/8=   4/11=   1/6=

8. (10)1/4=   5/5=   2/9=   2/3 =   3/5=

Name _____ Date _____

WRITING EQUIVALENT FRACTIONS BY DIVIDING 1
(Reducing or simplifying fractions)

DIRECTIONS: Write equivalent fractions by dividing the numerators and denominators by the greatest common factor (GCF). Hint: Try using the numerator as your divisor first.

Examples. 2/4 = ½ (The numerator and denominator can be divided equally by 2, the GCF.)

12/15 = 4/5 (The numerator and denominator can be divided by 3, the GCF)

If the numerator and denominator are the same, the fraction equals 1 whole.

Examples.   3/3 =1   4/4 =1   8/8 =1

1.	2/4=	16/18=	3/3=	8/10=	4/6=
2.	12/14=	6/8=	15/18=	6/16=	5/5=
3.	8/36=	4/8=	4/4=	3/9=	4/12=
4.	2/8=	9/27=	10/40=	6/48=	10/10=
5.	7/42=	36/81=	7/7=	32/64=	6/9=
6.	11/22=	28/35=	12/12=	8/12=	25/25=

Nettie Whitney Bailey

Name _____ Date _____

WRITING EQUIVALENT FRACTIONS BY DIVIDING 2
(Reducing or simplifying fractions)

DIRECTIONS: Write equivalent fractions by dividing the numerators and denominators by the greatest common factor (GCF). **Hint:** Try using the numerator as your divisor first.

Examples. 5/10 = ½ (The numerator and denominator can be divided equally by 5, the GCF.)

21/35 = 3/5 (The numerator and denominator can be divided by 7, the GCF.)

If the numerator and denominator are the same, the fraction equals 1 whole.

Examples.   3/3 = 1   4/4 = 1   8/8 = 1

1.	25/30=	3/12=	14/63=	9/9=	2/22=
2.	24/56=	17/17=	21/27=	9/15=	10/14=
3.	4/32=	4/44=	5/30=	8/18=	2/2=
4.	3/6=	40/45=	4/6=	16/20=	6/6=
5.	35/45=	11/66=	20/24=	8/8=	4/18=

Name _____ Date _____

The fractions below cannot be reduced and are described as being in lowest terms. The numerators and denominators cannot be divided equally by the same number.

2/9   3/5   5/7   7/9   4/9

3/7   1/3   1/8   4/11   1/6

DIRECTION: Write five other fractions that cannot be reduced or simplified.

_____   _____   _____   _____   _____

Name _____ Date _____

CHANGING IMPROPER FRACTIONS TO MIXED NUMBERS
(Reducing or simplifying fractions)

READ CAREFULLY. In order to reduce an improper fraction, divide the denominator into the numerator by estimating how many times the denominator can be divided into the numerator. (Use your times tables) If the remainder is 0, your answer will be a whole number.

Example. 30/6 = 5 (What number can I multiply 6 by and get 30?)

If the remainder is greater than zero, your answer will be a mixed number, a whole number and a fraction. The remainder will be the numerator, and the denominator will remain the same.

Example. 22/7= 3 1/7

DIRECTION: Change these improper fractions to whole numbers or mixed numbers.

1. 24/6=	2. 10/2=	3. 11/5=	4. 75/3=
5. 10/7=	6. 25/8=	7. 14/7=	8. 36/10=
9. 50/7=	10. 13/6=	11. 15/2=	12. 7/2=
13. 22/6=	14. 9/8=	15. 100/10=	

Name _____ Date _____

CHANGING MIXED NUMBERS TO IMPROPER FRACTIONS

READ CAREFULLY. When you change a mixed number to a fraction, multiply the whole number by the denominator and add the numerator. The denominator stays the same.

Examples.   4 ½   =9/2 6 2/3   = 20/3

DIRECTIONS: Change each mixed numeral to an improper fraction.

1. 2 ½ =   2. 6 3/4 =   3. 7 ½ =   4. 3 5/6 =

5. 10 4/7 =   6. 5 8/9 =   7. 12 5/12 =   8. 4 7/8 =

9. 1 2/3 =   10. 25 4/5 =   11. 7 2/9 =   12. 11 3/5 =

13. 17 5/6 =   14. 34 7/9 =   15. 25 7/10 =

Nettie Whitney Bailey

STEPS TO ADD AND SUBTRACT FRACTIONS WITH LIKE DENOMINATORS

Step 1   Write the fraction in vertical form.

Step 2   Add the numerators.

Step 3   Keep the denominators the same.

Step 4   Solve.

Step 5   Determine if the sum or difference can be reduced by finding an equivalent fraction using division.

Step 6   Simplify if necessary.

Examples.

$$\begin{array}{r} \frac{2}{4} \\ +\frac{1}{4} \\ \hline \frac{3}{4} \end{array} \qquad \begin{array}{r} \frac{5}{6} \\ -\frac{1}{6} \\ \hline \frac{4}{6} \end{array} = \frac{2}{3} \qquad \begin{array}{r} \frac{4}{5} \\ +\frac{3}{5} \\ \hline \frac{7}{5} \end{array} = 1\ 2/5$$

Name _____ Date _____

ADDING FRACTIONS WITH LIKE DENOMINATORS

DIRECTIONS: Solve and simplify (reduce to lowest terms).

1. $1/4 + 2/4 =$
2. $2/7 + 3/7 =$
3. $3/10 + 4/10 =$
4. $3/8 + 4/8 =$
5. $5/13 + 5/13 =$
6. $2/6 + 2/6 =$
7. $1/8 + 1/8 =$
8. $1/9 + 2/9 =$
9. $2/10 + 2/10 =$
10. $3/12 + 1/12 =$
11. $1/18 + 5/18 =$
12. $6/15 + 4/15 =$

13. $2/8 + 2/8 =$
14. $8/12 + 2/12 =$
15. $1/6 + 3/6 =$
16. $3/5 + 4/5 =$
17. $8/11 + 4/11 =$
18. $2/4 + 5/4 =$
19. $9/13 + 8/13 =$
20. $6/8 + 5/8 =$
21. $2/7 + 5/7 =$
22. $4/3 + 2/3 =$
23. $12/25 + 11/25 =$
24. $6/10 + 2/10 =$

Nettie Whitney Bailey

Name _____ Date _____

SUBTRACTING FRACTIONS WITH LIKE DENOMINATORS

DIRECTIONS: Solve and simplify (reduce to lowest terms).

1. 3/4 - 2/4 =
2. 5/6 - 2/6 =
3. 2/2 - ½ =
4. 7/9 - 2/9 =
5. 2/4 - 1/4 =
6. 6/7 - 1/7 =
7. 10/13 - 3/13 =
8. 3/5 - 1/5 =
9. 6/8 - 1/8 =
10. 3/7 - 2/7 =
11. 8/11 - 1/11 =
12. 4/9 - 3/9 =
13. 7/10 - 4/10 =

14. 9/13 - 4/13 =
15. 4/6 - 1/6 =
16. 7/8 - 1/8 =
17. 2/7 - 1/7 =
18. 8/10 - 3/10 =
19. 10/12 - 4/12 =
20. 12/18 - 9/18 =
21. 13/15 - 3/15 =
22. 7/8 - 6/8 =
23. 4/5 - 1/5 =
24. 10/25 - 5/25 =
25. 9/10 - 1/10 =

Name _____ Date _____

STEPS TO ADD AND SUBTRACT FRACTIONS WITH UNLIKE DENOMINATORS

Step 1   Write the fraction in vertical form.

Step 2   Find the LCD (Least Common Denominator) by

a. finding a number that can be divided into both denominators equally; try the smaller denominator first.

OR

b. multiplying the denominators.

Step 3   Multiply the numerators and denominators by the same number and write the equivalent fractions.

Step 4   Solve.

Step 5   Determine if the sum or difference can be simplified or reduced by finding an equivalent fraction using division.

Step 6   Simplify or reduce if necessary.

Examples.

$$\frac{2}{3} = \frac{4}{6}$$
$$+ \frac{1}{6} = \frac{1}{6}$$
$$\frac{5}{6}$$

$$\frac{4}{6} = \frac{12}{18}$$
$$+ \frac{3}{9} = \frac{6}{18}$$
$$= \frac{18}{18} = 1$$

Name _____ Date _____

ADDING FRACTIONS WITH UNLIKE DENOMINATORS 1

DIRECTIONS: Solve and simplify.

1. $3/4 + 2/8 =$
2. $5/6 + 2/12 =$
3. $2/4 + \frac{1}{2} =$
4. $7/9 + 2/18 =$
5. $3/16 + 2/8 =$
6. $6/7 + 1/14 =$
7. $10/26 + 3/13 =$
8. $3/20 + 1/5 =$
9. $6/8 + 10/40 =$
10. $2/28 + 3/7 =$
11. $1/11 + 8/33 =$
12. $4/54 + 3/9 =$
13. $7/10 + 1/70 =$

14. $9/13 + 9/39 =$
15. $4/21 + 1/7 =$
16. $7/9 + 10/45 =$
17. $4/8 + 4/24 =$
18. $6/36 + 3/9 =$
19. $4/4 + 12/12 =$
20. $8/12 + 2/24 =$
21. $10/13 + 4/39 =$
22. $1/21 + 2/7 =$
23. $5/10 + 5/20 =$
24. $4/6 + 6/36 =$
25. $7/7 + 12/56 =$

Name _____ Date _____

ADDING FRACTIONS WITH UNLIKE DENOMINATORS 2

DIRECTIONS: Solve and simplify.

1.   2/3 + 1/2 =
2.   1/2 + 2/7 =
3.   2/5 + 1/2 =
4.   2/3 + 4/5 =
5.   8/9 + 1/2 =
6.   2/5 + 2/6 =
7.   5/7 + 2/2 =
8.   2/5 + 4/7 =
9.   8/9 + 1/5 =
10. 5/6 + 2/5 =
11. 2/9 + 5/6 =
12. 2/8 + 6/12 =
13. 7/7 + 2/2 =

14. 6/3 + 1/2 =
15. 4/7 + 2/6 =
16. 2/3 + 4/8 =
17. 8/9 + 2/2 =
18. 1/5 + 1/6 =
19. 3/4 + 1/7 =
20. 1/5 + 6/12 =
21. 4/5 + 1/2 =
22. 2/3 + 1/4 =
23. 3/4 + 3/5 =
24. 2/9 + 4/12 =
25. 2/3 + 5/5 =

Nettie Whitney Bailey

Name _____ Date _____

ADDING AND SUBTRACTING FRACTIONS WITH LIKE AND UNLIKE DENOMINATORS

DIRECTIONS: Solve. Express your answer in simplest terms.

1. $2/5 + 3/5 =$

2. $5/7 + 2/3 =$

3. $3/10 + 7/15 =$

4. $8/24 + 16/24 =$

5. $2/13 + 8/13 =$

6. $2\ 3/5 + 8\ 1/10 =$

7. $4\ 3/9 + 4\ 3/9 =$

8. $9\ 2/3 + 7\ 2/4 =$

9. $20\ 6/11 + 20\ 2/11 =$

10. $2\ 5/9 + 2\ 3/18 =$

11. $6/7 - 3/7 =$

12. $5/6 - 3/12 =$

13. $16/24 - 8/24 =$

14. $13/13 - 11/13 =$

15. $25/25 - 10/25 =$

16. $19\ 8/10 - 11\ 4/5 =$

17. $17\ 19/26 - 11\ 6/26 =$

18. $35\ 7/3 - 5\ 4/7 =$

19. $100\ 18/40 - 50\ 2/40 =$

20. $7\ 9/24 - 1/24 =$

STEPS TO MULTIPLY FRACTIONS AND MIXED NUMBERS

Step 1.   Write the fraction in vertical form.

Step 2.   Check and see if the numerators and denominators diagonally opposite each other can be divided equally.

Step 2A.   If not, multiply the numerators then multiply the denominators and simplify.

Examples.

$$\frac{1}{2} \times \frac{1}{2} = \frac{1}{4} \qquad\qquad \frac{2}{3} \times \frac{4}{5} = \frac{8}{15}$$

$$\frac{2}{3} \times \frac{1}{5} = \frac{2}{15} \qquad\qquad \frac{1}{5} \times \frac{4}{6} = \frac{4}{30} = \frac{2}{15}$$

Step 2A.   If so, cancel (draw a line through the number) and divide. Multiply the new numerators then multiply the new denomina-tors and simplify.

Examples.

$$\frac{4}{5} \times \frac{\overset{1}{\cancel{3}}}{\underset{2}{\cancel{8}}} = \frac{3}{10} \qquad\qquad \frac{\overset{1}{\cancel{3}}}{\underset{3}{\cancel{6}}} \times \frac{\overset{1}{\cancel{2}}}{7} = \frac{3}{21} = \frac{1}{7}$$

$$\frac{\overset{2}{\cancel{4}}}{\underset{5}{\cancel{10}}} \times \frac{\overset{1}{\cancel{5}}}{\underset{3}{\cancel{6}}} = \frac{2}{15} \qquad\qquad \frac{\overset{1}{\cancel{4}}}{\underset{3}{\cancel{12}}} \times \frac{\overset{2}{\cancel{8}}}{\underset{4}{\cancel{16}}} = \frac{2}{12} = \frac{1}{6}$$

MIXED NUMBERS

Step 1   Change the mixed numbers to improper fractions.

Step 2   Check and see if the numerators and denominators opposite each other can be divided equally.

Step 2A.   If not, multiply the numerators then multiply the denominators, and simplify.

Examples.

$$6 \tfrac{1}{2} \times 6 \tfrac{1}{2} = \frac{13}{2} \times \frac{13}{2} = \frac{169}{4} = 42^{1/4}$$

Step 2B. If so, cancel (draw a line through the number) and divide. Multiply the new numerators then multiply the new denominators, and simplify.

$$\textit{Example. } 3\ 3/4 \times 4\ 2/5 = \frac{\overset{3}{\cancel{15}}}{\underset{2}{4}} \times \frac{\overset{11}{\cancel{22}}}{\cancel{5}} = \frac{33}{2} = 16\ \tfrac{1}{2}$$

Name _____ Date _____

MULTIPLYING FRACTIONS AND MIXED NUMBERS

DIRECTIONS: Solve and simplify.

1. 2/3 x 1/3 =
2. 3/4 x 1/2 =
3. 1/5 x 2/3 =
4. ½ x 3/5 =
5. 4/7 x 1/3 =
6. ½ x 1/3 =
7. 1/5 x 1/2 =
8. 7/10 x 3/7 =
9. 3/8 x ½ =
10. ½ x ½ =
11. 1/4 x 2/3 =
12. 3/10 x 5/7 =
13. 2/6 x 3/5 =

14. 4/5 x 1/8 =
15. 3/8 x 2/3 =
16. 6/8 x 2/3 =
17. 4/10 x 2/6 =
18. 12/15 x 3/4 =
19. 5/14 x 21/25 =
20. 4/9 x 18/20 =
21. 3 ½ x 3 ½ =
22. 2 4/5 x 1 3/4 =
23. 4 2/3 x 5 ½ =
24. 6 1/3 x 4 3/6 =
25. 8 8/10 x 6 4/11 =

STEPS TO DIVIDE FRACTIONS AND MIXED NUMBERS

Step 1 Write the fraction in vertical form.

Step 2 Write the reciprocal of the second fraction.

Examples. $\dfrac{4}{5} \div \dfrac{3}{7} = \dfrac{4}{5} \times \dfrac{7}{3}$

$\dfrac{2}{3} \div \dfrac{4}{5} = \dfrac{2}{3} \times \dfrac{5}{4}$

Step 3 Check and see if the numerators and denominators opposite each other can be divided equally.

Step 3A If not, multiply the numerators then multiply the denominators and simplify if necessary.

Example. $\dfrac{4}{5} \times \dfrac{7}{3} = \dfrac{28}{15} = 1\dfrac{13}{15}$

Step 3B. If so, cancel (draw a line through the number) and divide. Multiply the new numerators then multiply the new denominators, and simplify.

Examples. $\dfrac{2}{3} \div \dfrac{4}{5} = \dfrac{\cancel{2}^{1}}{3} \times \dfrac{5}{\cancel{4}_{2}} = \dfrac{5}{6}$

$\dfrac{2}{4} \div \dfrac{18}{24} = \dfrac{\cancel{2}}{4} \times \dfrac{\cancel{24}^{9}}{\cancel{18}_{1}} = \dfrac{6}{9} = \dfrac{2}{3}$

Name _____ Date _____

MIXED NUMBERS

Step 1.   Change the mixed numbers to improper fractions.

Step 2.   Write the reciprocal of the second fraction and prepare to multiply.

Examples. $6\ 2/3 \div 3\ 2/4 = \dfrac{20}{3} \div \dfrac{14}{4} = \dfrac{20}{3} \times \dfrac{4}{14} =$

$10\ ½ \div 2\ ½ = \dfrac{21}{2} \div \dfrac{5}{2} = \dfrac{21}{2} \times \dfrac{2}{5} =$

Step 3.   Check and see if the numerators and denominators opposite each other can be equally divided.

Step 3A.   If not, multiply the numerators then multiply the denominators, and simplify.

Examples. $6\ 2/3 \div 3\ 2/4 = \dfrac{20}{3} \div \dfrac{14}{4} = \dfrac{20}{3} \times \dfrac{4}{14} = \dfrac{80}{42} = 1\ 19/21$

Step 3B.   If so, cancel (draw a line through the number) and divide. Multiply the new numerators then multiply the new denominators, and simplify.

Example. $10\ ½ \div 2\ ½ = \dfrac{21}{2} \times \dfrac{5}{2} = \dfrac{21}{\overset{}{2}} \times \dfrac{\overset{1}{2}}{5} = \dfrac{21}{5} = 4\ 1/5$

Nettie Whitney Bailey

Name _____ Date _____

DIVIDING FRACTIONS AND MIXED NUMBERS

DIRECTIONS: Solve and simplify.

1. $3/4 \div 1/2 =$
2. $2/3 \div 1/2 =$
3. $1/5 \div 1/8 =$
4. $\frac{1}{2} \div \frac{1}{2} =$
5. $4/6 \div 1/3 =$
6. $6/9 \div 1/3 =$
7. $4/5 \div 1/10 =$
8. $8/10 \div 4/7 =$
9. $7/8 \div \frac{1}{2} =$
10. $5/6 \div 1/4 =$
11. $3/4 \div 2/3 =$
12. $7/10 \div 3/7 =$
13. $4/6 \div 4/5 =$

14. $4/5 \div 2/8 =$
15. $7/8 \div 2/3 =$
16. $6/8 \div 1/3 =$
17. $4/10 \div 2/6 =$
18. $8/12 \div 3/4 =$
19. $5/7 \div 3/5 =$
20. $4/9 \div 8/10 =$
21. $4\ \frac{1}{2} \div 4\ \frac{1}{2} =$
22. $4\ 3/6 \div 2\ 1/4 =$
23. $4\ 6/8 \div 2\ \frac{1}{2} =$
24. $8\ 2/3 \div 4\ 3/6 =$
25. $8\ 1/3 \div 6\ 1/4 =$

Name _____

NAMES OF DECIMALS

DIRECTIONS: Read the following sentences carefully. Study the examples. When you say the name of a decimal that has one numeral to the right of the decimal point, say the name of the numeral and the word "tenths". If there are two numerals to the right of the decimal point, even if one is a zero, say the name of the numeral and the word "hundredths". If there are three numerals to the right of the decimal point, even if there are zeroes, say the name of the numeral and the word "thousandths". If there are four numerals to the right of the decimal point, even if there are zeroes, say the name of the numeral and the words "ten thousandths". If there are 5 numerals to the right of the decimal point, even if there are zeroes, say the name of the numeral and the words "hundred thousandths"; etc.

Examples. .3 = three tenths
.25 = twenty-five hundredths
.09 = nine hundredths
.678 = six hundred seventy-eight thousandths
.032 = thirty-two thousandths
.005 = five thousandths
.2469 = two thousand, four hundred sixty-nine ten thousandths
.0305 = three hundred five ten thousandths
.12345 = twelve thousand, three hundred forty-five hundred thousandths
.20019 = twenty thousand, nineteen hundred thousandths

A decimal point after a numeral does not change the value of the numeral. *Examples.* 4. is the same as 4

15. is the same as 15

126. is the same as 126

When you say the name of a numeral that contains a whole number and a decimal, say the name of the first numeral, (the whole number) then the name of the decimal point, "and", and then the name of the second numeral and the word that describes the number of digits (tenths, hundredths, etc.).

Examples. 8.5 = eight and five tenths

35.46 = thirty-five and forty-six hundredths

Name _____ Date _____

WRITING THE NAMES OF DECIMALS

DIRECTION: Write the names of the decimals. Use your dictionary to check for correct spellings.

1.   4.   _____

2.   24.   _____

3.   155.   _____

4.   .2   _____

5.   .7   _____

6.   6.9   _____

7.   .15   _____

8.   .75   _____

9.   .07   _____

10. 3.09   _____

11. .238   _____

12. .067   _____

13. .001   _____

14. 3.801   _____

15. 245.100 _____

ADDING AND SUBTRACTING DECIMALS

Step 1. Write the numerals, one under the other, so that the decimal points are in a straight line.

Step 2. Put zeroes in places where there are no numerals.

Step 3. Solve.

Step 4. Put the decimal point in the sum or difference (the answer) directly under the decimal points in the problem.

Step 5. Check.

Example: Add   23,.7,.45,5

```
 23.00
   .70
   .45
  5.00
 29.15
```

Example: Subtract. 16.9 from 34.021

```
  34.021      16.900
 -16.900    + 17.121
  17.121      34.021
```

Name _____ Date _____

ADDING AND SUBTRACTING DECIMALS

DIRECTIONS. Add. Check your work. If you added the numerals from top to bottom to solve the problem, add them from bottom to top to check it.

1) 345. + 79. + 608. =   **2)** 258. + 369. + 111. =   **3)** .25 + .66 + .49 =

4) 7.28 + 3.19 =   **5)** .369 + .05 =   **6)** 705 + 716 + .22 =

DIRECTIONS. Subtract. Check your work by adding the subtrahend (the bottom numeral) and the difference (your answer). The sum of those two numerals will equal the minuend (the top number) if your answer is correct.

7) 601. - 55. =   **8)** 910. - 209. =   **9)** 34,006. - 13,455. =

10) 9.8 - 3.4 =   **11)** 717.34 - .28 =   **12)** 95 - .366 =

MULTIPLYING DECIMALS

Step 1. Solve.

Step 2. Count the number of numerals to the right of the decimal points in the problem.

Step 3. Place the decimal point in the product (answer) so that there are the same number of numerals to the right of the decimal point.

Step 4. Check.

Example: Multiply.

$$
\begin{array}{r}
9.137 \\
\times\ .25 \\
\hline
45685 \\
18274 \\
\hline
2.28425
\end{array}
$$

Name _____ Date _____

MULTIPLYING DECIMALS

DIRECTIONS. Solve and check.

1) 35
  x .9

2) 2.6
  x 4.7

3) 1.83
  x 2.51

4) 35.06
  x .53

5) 126
  x .621

6) .4005
  x 7.8

DIVIDING A DECIMAL BY A WHOLE NUMBER

Step 1. Rewrite the problem in usual form.

Step 2. Solve.

Step 3. Place the decimal point in the quotient (answer) directly over the

decimal point in the dividend.

Step 4. Check.

Example: $93.6 \div 7 = 13.4$ $13.4 \times 7 = 93.6$

DIVIDING A DECIMAL BY A DECIMAL

Step 1   Rewrite the problem in usual form.

Step 2. Change the divisor (number outside the box) to a whole number. Cross out the decimal point and move it to the right of the numeral in the ones place.

Step 3. Cross out the decimal point in the dividend and move it the same number of spaces to the right.

Step 4. Solve. Add zero(es) to avoid a remainder.

Step 5. Place the decimal point in the quotient (answer) directly over the decimal point in the dividend.

Step 6. Check.

Example: $4.2063 \div .21 =$ $420.63 \div 21 =$ $20.03 \times .21 =$

Name_____Date_____

DIVIDING DECIMALS BY WHOLE NUMBERS AND DECIMALS

DIRECTIONS. Solve and check.

1) $1.8 \div 3 =$ **2)** $63.9 \div 9 =$ **3)** $625.05 \div 5 =$

4) $7.1024 \div 16 =$ **5)** $2135.10 \div 30 =$ **6)** $635.46 \div 238 =$

7) $.35 \div .7 =$ **8)** $4.08 \div .8 =$ **9)** $1.45 \div .2 =$

10) $400.5 \div 1.5 =$ **11)** $64.848 \div .24 =$ **12)** $.1612 \div .62 =$

Name_____Date_____

DECIMAL/FRACTION REVIEW

DIRECTIONS. Read carefully. Write, solve, and check.

1. Write an addition problem using these numerals:
    .4, 39, 6.37, .001
2. Write a subtraction problem using these numerals:
    1.26 and 300.23
3. Write a multiplication problem using these numerals:
    34.5 & .50
4. Write a division problem using these numerals:
    4.863 &3
5. Write the factors of:

    8 _____13 _____
    20_____35 _____
    56 _____

6. Write one fraction using these numerals: 4 & 6
    Which one is the numerator?_____
    Which one is the denominator?_____

7. Simplify the fraction you wrote for #6. Show your work:

9. Write a different fraction using these numerals: 4 & 6 Which one is
the numerator?_____

Name _____

Which one is the denominator?_____

9. Simplify the fraction.

Show your work:

10 Which fraction is larger, 3/4 or 6/8? Prove your answer.

Show your work:

DIRECTIONS. Solve. Simplify. Show your work.

11) 1/3 + 2/3 =   **12)** 2/5 + 3/10 =   **13)** 7/12 - 2/6 =

14) 3/4 + 2/3 =   **15)** 5 6/9 - 1/6 =   **16)** 3/4 x 2/9 =

17) 8/14 x 2/24 =   **18)** 4/6 ÷ 3.4 =   **19)** 5 7/8 ÷ 3/4 =

Name _____ Date _____

FRACTIONS, DECIMALS, PER CENTS

Changing fractions to decimals.

> ***Hint:*** Write an equivalent fraction with 100 as the denominator. Write the decimal.

Changing decimals to per cents.

> ***Hint:*** Remove the decimal point and add per cent sign.

Changing percentages to fractions.

> ***Hint:*** Remove per cent sign and add denominator of 100.

Name _____ Date _____

DIRECTIONS. Complete the chart. Show your work.

Fractions	Decimals	Percentages
		50%
	0.33	
1/4		
		20%
	0.75	
1/10		
		66%
	0.125	
4/5		
2/3		
		35%
	0.15	
25/5		
		100%

Name _____ Date _____

MEASURING TIME

DIRECTIONS. Fill in the blanks. Don't guess. Use a calendar and your dictionary.

1. There are _____ days in a week.

2. There are _____ days in a school week.

3. There are _____ weeks in a month.

4. The months of _____, _____, _____, and _____ have _____ days. All the rest, _____, _____, _____, _____, _____, _____, _____ have _____ days, except _____, which has _____ days, except in leap year when it has _____ days.

5. There are _____ days in a regular year.

6. . There are _____ days in leap year which comes every _____ years.

7. There are _____ weeks in a year.

8. There are _____ months in a year.

9. There are _____ years in a decade.

10. There are _____ years in a score.

11. There are _____ years in a century.

12. There are _____ years in a millennium.

Name _____ Date _____

UNITS OF DISTANCE

Remember: 12 inches (in.) = 1 foot (ft.)   3 feet = 1 yard (yd.)
                36 inches (in.) = 1 yard (yd.)

Questions you must ask yourself and answer before you solve these
problems: 1. How many _____s are in one _____?
              2. Am I changing a small unit to a larger unit?
              3. Am I changing a large unit to a smaller unit?
              4. What operation (+, x,÷) do I use to solve this problem?

Hints: If you have to change a small unit to a larger unit, divide.
        If you have to change a large unit to a smaller unit, multiply

Example.   3 feet = _____ inches
             There are 12 inches in 1 foot.
             I'm changing a large unit to a smaller unit so I multiply.
             3 x 12 = 36 in.

DIRECTIONS. Read each problem, answer the questions, then solve
each problem. Show your work and number each problem.

1. 3 yards = _____ feet

2. 8 yards = _____ feet

3. 1 yard = _____ inches

4. 2 yards = _____ inches

5. 21 feet = _____ yards

5. 12 feet = _____ yards

6. 5 yards = _____ feet

7. 14 yards = _____ feet

8. 3 yards = _____ feet

9. 3 feet = _____ inches

10. 7 yards = _____ feet

11. 9 feet = _____ inches

12. 18 feet = _____ yards

13. 11 yards = _____ feet

14. 9 yards = _____ feet

15. 5 feet = _____ inches

16. 7 feet = _____ inches

17. 27 feet = _____ yards

18. 6 yards = _____ feet

19. 15 feet = _____ yards

20. 9 feet = _____ yards

21. 10 yards = _____ feet

HELPFUL HINTS TO SOLVE STORY/WORD PROBLEMS

Make this a part of the mathematics bulletin board or give each child a copy.

Name_____

STORY/WORD PROBLEMS
HELPFUL HINTS

1. Always read the problem carefully and get a mental picture of what is happening, what is taking place. Think, and try to remember if you have ever had a similar experience.

2. Identify exactly what you are being asked to find.

3. Identify the information that you DO NOT need to solve the problem. (Ask yourself, if this wasn't in the problem, could I still find what the problem is asking me to find?)

4. Identify all the information that you NEED to help you solve the problem.

5. Identify clues that help you figure out whether to add, subtract, multiply, or divide.

   a. Clues that tell you to subtract: How many are left? Find the difference between? How much more?
   b. Clues that tell you to add: all together, total, in all, sum
   c. Multiply when you are asked to change a larger quantity (amount) to a smaller quantity (amount).
   d. Divide when you are asked to change a smaller quantity (amount) to a larger quantity (amount).
   e. Solve the problem, check your work, and label your answer.

Name _____

Checking your work:

Addition problems:

If you first added from top to bottom, check your work by adding from bottom to top.

Subtraction problems:

Add the difference (the answer) and bottom number (the subtrahend). If the sum (the total) of those 2 numbers is the same as the top number (the minuend), your answer is correct. If you get a different number, your answer is wrong. Work the problem again to find your mistake.

Multiplication problems:

Reverse the numbers that you multiplied and see if you get the same answer.

> *Example:* 89 x 7 =
>
> Solve: 9 x 7 = ; 8 x 7 =
>
> Check: 7 x 9 =; 7 x 8

Division problems:

Multiply the quotient (answer) by the divisor (the number outside the box). The product (answer) should be the same as the dividend (the number inside the box) plus the remainder if there is one. If you get a different answer, go back and work the problem again to find your mistake.

ROMAN NUMERALS

This can be used as a part of your math bulletin board. Use the page numbers to teach/practice Roman numerals.

ROMAN NUMERALS

i = 1

v = 5

x = 10

l = 50

c = 100

Combine letters to express all numbers.

Examples.

iii = 3
xxx = 30 (10 + 10 + 10 = 30)
iv = 4 (5 - 1 = 4)
ix = 9 (10 - 1 = 9)
xl = 40
xc = 90

Name _____ Date _____

STATES IN THE UNITED STATES OF AMERICA

Group I (1)

DIRECTIONS. Write the names of the states in alphabetical order that begin with the letters shown below. The numbers in parentheses tell how many states there are whose names begin with that letter. Use a map, a dictionary, an encyclopedia, a gazetteer, or a social science or geography book to get the correct spellings.

A (4)	C (3)	D (1)	F (1)	G (1)

_____

_____

_____

_____

_____

_____

_____

_____

_____

Name _____ Date _____

STATES IN THE UNITED STATES OF AMERICA

Group II (2)

DIRECTIONS. Write the names of the states in alphabetical order that begin with the letters shown below. The numbers in parentheses tell how many states there are whose names begin with that letter. Use a map, a dictionary, an encyclopedia, a gazetteer, or a social science or geography book to get the correct spellings.

H (1)   I (4)   K (2)   L (1)   M (8)

_____
_____
_____
_____
_____
_____
_____
_____
_____
_____
_____
_____
_____
_____
_____
_____

Name _____ Date _____

STATES IN THE UNITED STATES OF AMERICA

Group III (3)

DIRECTIONS. Write the names of the states in alphabetical order that begin with the letters shown below. The numbers in parentheses tell how many states there are whose names begin with that letter. Use a map, a dictionary, an encyclopedia, a gazetteer, or a social science or geography book to get the correct spellings.

N (8)   O (3)   P (1)   R (1)   S (2)

_____

_____

_____

_____

_____

_____

_____

_____

_____

_____

_____

_____

_____

_____

_____

Name _____ Date _____

STATES IN THE UNITED STATES OF AMERICA

Group IV (4)

DIRECTIONS. Write the names of the states in alphabetical order that begin with the letters shown below. The numbers in parentheses tell how many states there are whose names begin with that letter. Use a map, a dictionary, an encyclopedia, a gazetteer, or a social science or geography book to get the correct spellings.

T(2)   U (1)   V (1)   W (4)

_____

_____

_____

_____

_____

_____

_____

_____

Name _____ Date _____

CONTINENTS

A continent is a very, very, very large piece of land. There are seven (7) continents in the world.

DIRECTIONS. Unscramble the name of a continent and the three countries on it.

1. tornh icerama _____

   adanac _____

   ocixem _____

   edutin ssaett fo icerama _____

DIRECTIONS. Unscramble the names of the other six continents. Read the descriptions. Write the number of the continent in front of its description.

1. icarcatant _____

2. sailaurat _____

3. caraif _____

4. aais _____

5. poreeu _____

6. houst icemara _____

Name _____

____ This continent is where kangaroos, duckbill platypuses, and koala bears live in the wild. (If someone asks what a duckbill platypus is, tell them that it is one of the strangest animals in all the world and challenge them to look it up the next time they go to the library.

____ This continent is all ice and snow. Polar bears, penguins, and walruses live there but no inhabitants (people).

____ This continent is where most of the pyramids are located (some are in Mexico), where Nelson Mandela was in jail for almost thirty (30) years, and where slave traders got most of the slaves from that were brought to this and other countries. It's where you can go on safari and see elephants, lions, hippos, and lots of other jungle animals.

____ When we're having winter on our continent, the people on this continent are having summer. Some people who drink coffee have probably enjoyed coffee that was grown in Brazil or Colombia, two of the countries on this continent. This is where you can go to see rain forests and the Andes Mountains.

____ This is the continent where you could go and visit Russia. It's also where most Chinese and Japanese people live and lots of Indians, but not the same kinds of Indians that live in the United States and helped the Pilgrims.

____ You can go to this continent and see the Eiffel Tower in Paris, France, Pope John Paul II at the Vatican in Italy, and scenes of the Holocaust, during which six million (6,000,000) Jews were killed.

ANSWERS

I LANGUAGE ARTS

DOLCH WORDS 1

Section I

1 know	5 what	3 ride	3 don't	1 after
5 your	1 carry	5 with	4 make	3 fast
3 ran	3 his	2 find	5 of	5 out
2 may	4 put	4 stop	2 came	4 funny
4 under	2 give	1 am	1 but	2 as

Section II

1 has	5 will	5 went	1 cold	3 fly
2 have	3 here	1 from	4 over	2 call
4 some	1 five	2 help	5 six	4 it
5 who	4 small	4 soon	2 did	1 buy
3 if	2 going	3 so	3 get	5 that

Section III

1 all	5 ten	5 run	1 at	4 was
2 away	4 my	1 around	4 said	1 black
5 this	3 eat	4 one	5 three	3 green
4 little	1 an	3 on	3 not	5 yes
3 her	2 be	2 come	2 him	2 brown

DOLCH WORDS 1a

I		II		III		IV		V	
7	know	14	what	9	ride	6	don't	1	after
15	your	3	carry	15	with	9	make	7	fast
10	ran	9	his	4	find	11	of	12	out
9	may	11	put	13	stop	3	came	9	funny
13	under	6	give	1	am	2	but	2	as
3	has	15	will	14	went	4	cold	8	fly
4	have	8	here	5	from	12	over	6	call
11	some	5	five	6	help	14	six	11	its
14	who	12	small	12	soon	5	did	5	buy
6	if	7	going	11	so	7	get	13	that
1	all	13	ten	10	run	1	at	14	was
2	away	10	my	2	around	13	said	3	black
12	this	4	eat	8	one	15	three	10	green
8	little	1	an	7	on	10	not	15	yes
5	her	2	be	3	one	8	him	4	brown

Nettie Whitney Bailey

DOLCH WORDS 2

Section I

3 like	1 are	2 good	1 can	4 you
1 a	4 look	4 no	3 go	2 me
5 yellow	5 saw	3 is	5 she	1 had
4 old	2 blue	5 see	2 for	5 up
2 in	3 down	1 and	4 he	3 play

Section II

4 into	3 start	3 its	3 the	2 done
5 jump	5 to	5 use	2 red	4 two
2 full	2 big	4 too	5 wash	5 we
3 I	1 ate	2 hurt	1 own	3 shall
1 because	4 these	1 first	4 those	1 do

Section III

5 wish	2 never	3 kind	2 best	1 been
4 try	5 were	1 clean	1 any	5 read
2 better	3 show	2 found	4 thank	4 does
3 far	4 want	4 much	5 think	2 bring
1 always	1 fall	5 which	3 got	3 could

DOLCH WORDS 2a

	I		II		III		IV		V
11	like	1	are	5	good	3	can	15	you
1	a	7	look	11	no	5	go	8	me
15	yellow	9	saw	7	is	10	she	7	had
12	old	4	blue	12	see	4	for	13	up
8	in	5	down	1	and	7	he	9	play
9	into	11	start	8	its	12	the	6	done
10	jump	13	to	14	use	9	red	12	two
6	full	3	big	13	too	15	wash	14	we
7	I	2	ate	6	hurt	8	own	11	shall
3	because	12	these	3	first	14	those	4	do
14	wish	8	never	9	kind	2	best	1	been
13	try	15	were	2	clean	1	any	10	read
4	better	10	show	4	found	11	thank	5	does
5	far	14	want	10	much	13	think	2	bring
2	always	6	fall	15	which	6	got	3	could

DOLCH WORDS 3

Section I

2	gave	1	draw	1	goes	2	pick	3	off
5	pull	4	only	2	grow	4	their	2	light
1	four	3	keep	4	open	3	tell	1	how
3	hot	5	us	5	well	5	would	4	together
4	new	2	hold	3	once	1	again	5	very

Section II

2	live	3	right	4	sing	2	laugh	3	seven
1	ask	4	warm	2	made	1	about	1	many
3	or	1	just	3	say	3	long	4	take
5	they	5	white	1	every	4	round	5	today
4	then	2	our	5	when	5	write	2	pretty

Section III

5	upon	2	let	1	before	3	must
3	sit	4	them	5	where	5	work
1	cut	1	both	3	myself	1	by
4	these	3	sleep	2	drink	4	why
2	now	5	walk	4	please	2	eight

DOLCH WORDS 3a

I		II		III		IV		V	
4	gave	2	draw	4	goes	7	pick	5	off
9	pull	7	only	5	grow	10	their	3	light
3	four	5	keep	9	open	9	tell	2	how
5	hot	12	us	12	well	13	would	11	together
7	new	3	hold	8	once	2	again	12	very
6	live	9	right	11	sing	4	laugh	8	seven
1	ask	13	warm	6	made	1	about	4	many
8	or	4	just	10	say	5	long	9	take
13	they	14	white	3	every	8	round	10	today
11	then	8	our	13	when	14	write	7	pretty
14	upon	6	let	1	before	6	must	1	eight
10	sit	11	them	14	where	12	work	6	please
2	cut	1	both	7	myself	3	by	13	walk
12	there	10	sleep	2	drink	11	why		

Name _____ Date _____

CAPITALIZATION & PUNCTUATION

1. Does your dog like to chase cats?

2. Her cousin Keli graduated from eighth grade.

3. Room 213 went to the Planetarium.

4. What street does your uncle live on?

5. Watch out for that car!

6. The mailman delivers the mail at 1000 A. M. every morning.

7. Lots of people love Mayor Johnson.

8. When my Aunt Jane calls me, she always opens our conversations with, "Hello, how was your day?"

9. Mr. Robins told his class that he saw the movie Titanic ten times.

10. Sarah's favorite book is Mamma I Wanna Sing.

CONTRACTIONS I

1. He is

He is going to Disney World for his birthday.

2. can not

My mother can not drive a car with a stick shift.

3. We are

We are going to read two books every week.

4. I am

I am going to be late for school.

5 would not

My father would not let us watch WWF last night.

6. couldn't

7. I'll

8. she's

9. we've

10. they're

CONTRACTIONS 2

1. He is	He is going to the store.
2. can not	My two-year old brother can not tie his shoes.
3. We are	We are going to finish all of our homework.
4. I am	I am going to be late for school.
5. would not	Sam would not eat because he does not like oatmeal.
6. I have	I am out of breath because I have been running.
7. She will	She will bite you if you bother her puppies.
8. will not	The baby will not eat because he is sick.
9. could not	My grandmother could not find her umbrella.
10. They are	They are going to Pete's birthday party.
11. did not	She got in trouble because she did not wash the dishes.
12. I will	I will watch Barney with my little sister tomorrow morning.
13. were not	There were not any cars parked on the street.
14. should not	You should not do your math problems with a pen.
15. have not	I have not been to the show to see Mulan yet.
16. do not	Michelle, do not drink all the milk.
17. does not	Mary does not want to go shopping.

NOUNS, VERBS, AND ADJECTIVES *2*

person, place, thing

action or a state of being

describes looks, hears, smells, feels, tastes (Any order is acceptable.)

1. type v.	2. fine adj.	3. shade n.	4. watch v.
5. box v.	6. train v.	7. park, swing n. v.	
8. wave v.	9. paint, back v. adj.	10. park v.	
11. type n.	12. fine n.	13. shade v.	
14. paint, swing n. n.	15. train n.	16. pipe n.	
17. watch n.	18. wave n.	19. back n.	20. pipe v.

we, we, our, My, I, you, you, my, I, I, her, I, my, her, you, your, you, you, you, who, his, her, we, we. our, I, my, his, he, who, his, they, they, their, their

NOUNS, PRONOUNS, VERBS, AND ADJECTIVES

Adjective	Noun	Verb	Pronoun
1. extra	Mr. Green, credit, report	said, can, get, type	we, we, our
2. Tony's good	report, job	read, said, had done	he, he, he
3. couch	shade, sun, cover	pull, won't, fade	
4.	Mama, plant	said, be, watch, doing, don't, knock, pull	you're, you, my, you, it
5.	Muhammad Ali, person	wish, could have, seen, box	I, I
6.	hours	had, train	he
7.	Susan, brother, Judy, park	took, swing	her
8. baby	sister, Judy, bye-bye	taught, wave	her
9. back	Mrs. Williams, Tony, porch	wants, paint	her
10. good	dollars, job	promised, pay, does	she, him, he
11. driving	test, car	take, have, park	you, your, you
12.	type, vehicle, license	drive, determines, need	you, you
13. brown, nice	suit, Mr. Jordan, shade	bought	
14. porch, same	swing, color	plans, paint	he, his
15.	train, grandparents	going, take, visit	we, we, our
16.	tobacco, grandfather, pipe	like, smell, smokes	I, my, his

17. waterproof	Jesse, watch, graduation, surfing	received, likes, go	he
18. experienced, huge	surfer, wave	hopes, become, ride	he`
19. Reynolds, tired, fast, big	family, noise, pace, city	grew	
20. rural, star-studded,	area, sky, pollution, view	moved, able, see, hide	they, them

SINGULAR, PLURAL, & POSSESSIVE NOUNS

PRONOUN CONTRACTIONS

1. girls
2. They'll
3. girls'
4. Julie
5. Julie's
6. boys
7. boys'
8. they'll
9. George
10. He's
11. George's
12. She's

EIGHT PARTS OF SPEECH

1. Common nouns name any person, any place, or any thing.

   Proper nouns name specific persons, places and things.

2. A pronoun is a word that can take the place of a noun.

3. A verb is an action word or one that shows a state of being.

4. An adjective is a word that describes.

5. An adverb is a word that describes a verb, an adjective or another adverb.

6. A conjunction is a word that joins words, phrases, clauses, or sentences.

7. A preposition is a word that indicates position.

8. An interjection is a word that expresses strong feeling.

9. A noun marker, sometimes called an article, is a word that precedes a noun.

DIRECTED READING LESSON

(PRONOUN ANTECEDENTS)

1. volcano
2. dust and debris
3. humans
4. rescue workers
5. internists
6. internists
7. patients
8. volcanic dust
9. patients
10. doctors
11. doctors
12. doctors
13. doctors
14. patients
15. disease
16. dust particles

II MATHEMATICS

ADDITION FACTS 1

1.	11	13	12	10	12	11	12	10	13	11	13	13	12
2.	12	13	13	11	13	10	12	11	12	10	12	13	11
3.	11	13	10	12	10	13	10	13	11	13	12	11	12
4.	11	13	12	10	12	11	12	10	13	11	13	13	12
5.	12	13	13	11	13	10	12	11	12	10	12	13	11
6.	11	13	10	12	10	13	10	13	11	13	12	11	12

1A

1.	0	5	3	8
2.	2	4	6	1
3.	3	5	6	4
4.	8	12	11	9
5.	6	5	9	8
6.	0	3	7	9
7.	6	10	9	10
8.	10	7	2	0
9.	11	9	7	3
10.	11	10	3	11
11.	2	10	7	0
12.	13	13	11	0
13.	3	3	1	6
14.	9	9	10	5
15.	9	9	7	6

ADDITION FACTS 2

1.	10	13	12	14	12	11	14	10	13	11	10	13	12
2.	12	13	10	11	13	14	14	11	12	10	12	14	11
3.	11	10	13	12	14	12	11	13	14	14	10	10	10
4.	13	14	10	13	11	12	11	14	11	10	10	13	10
5.	11	13	12	10	14	11	12	10	13	14	13	10	12
6.	10	13	12	11	14	10	12	11	10	14	13	14	10

2A

1.	0	7	1	9
2.	8	3	6	3
3.	0	7	6	2
4.	9	12	9	3
5.	4	5	13	11
6.	3	6	11	3
7.	9	11	11	7
8.	9	9	7	11
9.	13	12	0	14
10.	10	7	5	11
11.	10	9	9	7
12.	6	8	2	0
13.	3	2	7	1
14.	9	2	2	11
15.	9	4	7	4

ADDITION FACTS 3

1.	15	13	14	15	11	12	15	11	14	12	13	15	14
2.	11	14	15	10	10	15	13	15	13	14	14	15	14
3.	15	14	13	15	14	15	11	10	11	15	15	11	15
4.	15	10	15	14	15	14	11	11	15	10	15	14	15
5.	11	14	15	10	10	15	15	10	12	10	15	15	10
6.	15	10	11	11	15	10	11	10	15	15	10	15	11

3A

1.	7	5	9	3
2.	1	9	3	6
3.	8	9	10	5
4.	9	7	10	13
5.	3	7	7	4
6.	10	10	12	9
7.	13	11	12	9
8.	7	14	8	1
9.	14	8	5	13
10.	0	2	8	8
11.	3	9	1	3
12.	1	1	11	7
13.	14	13	9	6
14.	12	0	8	7
15.	3	4	15	11

ADDITION FACTS 4

1.	16	13	12	10	16	15	11	10	13	16	15	12	16
2.	16	13	16	15	14	10	16	10	10	16	12	15	11
3.	13	16	16	12	12	12	16	14	14	14	16	16	10
4.	16	14	13	16	16	10	11	12	16	16	10	12	16
5.	15	16	16	11	11	10	16	10	16	12	16	16	12
6.	16	14	16	13	16	10	14	16	12	16	12	11	16

4A

1.	7	5	9	5
2.	1	9	3	6
3.	11	9	10	5
5.	3	9	7	4
4.	9	7	10	13
6.	10	10	12	9
7.	13	11	12	9
8.	7	14	10	1
9.	15	8	5	13
10.	0	2	8	9
11.	3	9	1	3
12.	1	1	11	7
13.	14	14	9	6
14.	12	0	8	7
15.	3	4	16	11

Nettie Whitney Bailey

ADDITION FACTS 5

1.	17	12	11	14	15	13	12	10	10	11	13	15	17
2.	11	13	16	10	10	10	13	11	12	10	16	14	11
3.	10	13	10	12	10	13	17	13	11	13	12	17	12
4.	16	13	12	13	14	15	16	10	12	16	17	15	17
5.	10	10	14	15	13	10	17	17	11	13	16	12	10
6.	13	16	17	15	17	10	17	14	12	17	10	17	12

5A

1.	4	8	4	7
2.	7	11	10	0
3.	3	5	10	7
4.	12	12	8	3
5.	9	6	16	13
6.	1	5	14	7
7.	7	7	11	10
8.	0	15	9	12
9.	0	10	7	8
10.	10	2	14	0
11.	2	5	8	9
12.	6	10	16	5
13.	0	14	8	7
14.	15	11	8	3
15.	10	6	11	4

ADDITION FACTS 6

1.	18	12	11	14	15	13	12	10	18	11	13	15	17
2.	11	13	16	10	18	10	13	11	12	10	16	14	18
3.	10	13	18	12	10	13	17	13	11	18	12	17	18
4.	16	13	12	13	14	18	16	10	12	16	17	15	18
5.	18	10	14	15	13	10	18	17	11	13	16	12	10
6.	13	18	17	15	17	10	18	14	12	17	10	18	13

6A

1.	6	8	5	12
2.	8	9	12	0
3.	8	12	6	3
4.	9	17	14	6
5.	11	17	9	16
6.	7	11	7	4
7.	12	10	15	12
8.	10	7	9	12
9.	9	11	9	8
10.	11	11	7	3
11.	5	5	8	4
12.	10	9	7	6
13.	1	1	17	13
14.	15	7	15	7
15.	11	1	14	12

ADDITION/MULTIPLICATION 1

1. 0   2. 0, 0   3. 0, 0   4. 0, 0, 0

5. 0, 0, 0, 0   6. 0, 0, 0, 0, 0   7. 0, 0, 0, 0, 0, 0

8. 0, 0, 0, 0, 0, 0, 0   9. 0, 0, 0, 0, 0, 0, 0, 0   10. 0, 0, 0, 0, 0, 0, 0, 0, 0, 0

11. 0, 0, 0, 0, 0, 0, 0, 0, 0, 0   12. 0, 0, 0, 0, 0, 0, 0, 0, 0, 0, 0

13. 0, 0, 0, 0, 0, 0, 0, 0, 0, 0, 0, 0

0, 0, 0 0, 0, 0 0, 0, 0 0, 0, 0 0	0, 0, 0 0, 0, 0 0, 0, 0 0, 0, 0 0
0, 0, 0 0, 0, 0 0, 0, 0 0, 0, 0 0	0, 0, 0 0, 0, 0 0, 0, 0 0, 0, 0 0

ADDITION/MULTIPLICATION 2

1. 0, 0	2. 1, 1, 1	3. 1, 2, 2	4. 1, 2, 3, 3
5. 1, 2, 3, 4, 4	6. 1, 2, 3, 4, 5, 5		7. 1, 2, 3, 4, 5, 6, 6
8. 1, 2, 3, 4, 5, 6, 7, 7		9. 1, 2, 3, 4, 5, 6, 7, 8, 8	
10. 1, 2, 3, 4, 5, 6, 7, 8, 9, 9		11. 1, 2, 3, 4, 5, 6, 7, 8, 9, 10, 10	
12. 1, 2, 3, 4, 5, 6, 7, 8, 9, 10, 11, 11			
13. 1, 2, 3, 4, 5, 6, 7, 8, 9, 10, 11, 12, 12			

0, 1, 2 3, 4, 5 6, 7, 8 9,10,11 12	0, 1, 2 3, 4, 5 6, 7, 8 9, 10, 11 12
0, 1, 2 3, 4, 5 6, 7, 8 9, 10, 11 12	0, 1, 2 3, 4, 5 6, 7, 8 9, 10, 11 12

ADDITION/MULTIPLICATION 3

1. 0, 0   2. 1, 2, 2   3. 2, 4, 4   4. 3, 6, 6
5. 4, 8, 8   6. 5, 10, 10   7. 6, 12, 12   8. 7, 14, 14
9. 8, 16, 16   10. 9, 18, 18   11. 10, 20, 20   12. 11, 22, 22
13. 12, 24, 24

0, 2, 4, 6, 8, 10, 12, 14, 16, 18, 20, 22, 24	0, 2, 4, 6, 8, 10, 12, 14, 16, 18, 20, 22 24
0, 2, 4, 6, 8, 10, 12, 14, 16, 18, 20, 22, 24	0, 2, 4, 6, 8, 10, 12, 14, 16, 18, 20, 22, 24

ADDITION/MULTIPLICATION 4

1, 0, 0, 0, 0   2. 1, 2, 3, 3   3. 2, 4, 6, 6   4. 3, 6, 9, 9
5. 4, 8, 12, 12   6. 5, 10, 15, 15   7. 6, 12, 18, 18
8. 7, 14, 21, 21   9. 8, 16, 24, 24   10. 9, 18, 27, 27
11. 10, 20, 30, 30   12. 11, 22, 33, 33   13. 12, 24, 36, 36

0, 3, 6 9, 12, 15 18, 21, 24 36	0, 3, 6 9, 12, 15 18, 21, 24 36
0, 3, 6 9, 12, 15 18, 21, 24 36	0, 3, 6 9, 12, 15 18, 21, 24 36

ADDITION/MULTIPLICATION 5

1. 0, 0, 0, 0, 0   2. 1, 2, 3, 4, 4   3. 2, 4, 6, 8, 8
4. 3, 6, 9, 12, 12   5. 4, 8, 12, 16, 16   6. 5, 10, 15, 20, 20
7. 6, 12, 18, 24, 24   8. 7, 14, 21, 28, 28   9. 8, 16, 24, 32, 32
10. 9, 18, 27, 36, 36   11. 10, 20, 30, 40, 40 12. 11, 22, 33, 44, 44
13, 12, 24, 36, 48, 48

0, 4, 8 12, 16, 20 24, 28, 32 36, 40, 44 48	0, 4, 8 12, 16, 20 24, 28, 32 36, 40, 44 48
0, 4, 8 12, 16, 20 24, 28, 32 36, 40, 44 48	0, 4, 8 12, 16, 20 24, 28, 32 36, 40, 44 48

ADDITION/MULTIPLICATION 6

1. 0, 0, 0, 0, 0, 0	2. 1. 2, 3, 4, 5, 5	3. 2, 4, 6, 8, 10,10
4. 3, 6, 8, 10, 12, 15	5. 4, 8, 12, 16, 20, 20	
6. 5, 10, 15, 20, 25, 25	7. 6, 12, 18, 24, 30, 30	
8. 7, 14, 21, 28, 35, 35	9. 8, 16, 24, 32, 40, 40	
10. 9, 18, 27, 36, 45, 45	11. 10, 20, 30, 40, 50, 50	
12. 11, 22, 33, 44, 55, 55	13. 12, 24, 36, 48, 60, 60	

0, 5, 10 15, 20, 25 30, 35, 40 45, 50, 55 60	0, 5, 10 15, 20, 25 30, 35, 40 45, 50, 55 60
0, 5, 10 15, 20, 25 30, 35, 40 45, 50, 55 60	0, 5, 10 15, 20, 25 30, 35, 40 45, 50, 55 60

ADDITION/MULTIPLICATION 7

1. 0, 0, 0, 0, 0, 0, 0   2. 1, 2, 3, 4, 5, 6, 6   3. 2, 4, 6, 8, 10, 12, 12

4. 3, 6, 9, 12, 15, 18, 18   5. 4, 8, 12, 16, 20, 24, 24

6. 5, 10, 15, 20, 25, 30, 30   7. 6, 12, 18, 24, 30, 36, 36

8. 7, 14, 21, 28, 35, 42, 42   9. 8, 16, 24, 32, 40, 48, 48

10. 9, 18, 27, 36, 45, 54, 54   11. 10, 20, 30, 40, 50, 60, 60

12. 11, 22, 33, 44, 55, 66, 66   13. 12, 24, 36, 48, 60, 72, 72

0, 6, 12 18, 24, 30 36, 42, 48, 54, 60, 66, 70	0, 6, 12 18, 24, 30 36, 42, 48, 54, 60, 66, 70
0, 6, 12 18, 24, 30 36, 42, 48, 54 60, 66, 70	0, 6, 12 18, 24, 30 36, 42, 48, 54 60, 66, 70

ADDITION/MULTIPLICATION 8

1. 0, 0, 0, 0, 0, 0, 0, 0   2. 1, 2, 3, 4, 5, 6, 7, 7   , 4, 6, 8, 10, 12, 14, 14

4. 3, 6, 9, 12, 15, 18, 21, 21   5. 4, 8, 12, 16, 20. 24, 28, 28
6. 5, 10, 15, 20, 25, 30, 35, 35   7. 6, 12, 18, 24, 30, 36, 42, 42
8. 7, 14, 21, 28, 35, 42, 49, 49   9. 8, 16, 24, 32, 40, 48, 56, 56
10. 9, 18, 27, 36, 45, 54, 63, 63   11. 10, 20, 30, 40, 50, 60, 70, 70
12. 11, 22, 33, 44, 55, 66, 77, 77   13. 12, 24, 36, 48, 60, 72, 84, 84

0, 7, 14 21, 28, 35 42, 49, 56, 63, 70, 77, 84	0, 7, 14 21, 28, 35 42, 49, 56, 63, 70, 77, 84
0, 7, 14 21, 28, 35 42, 49, 56, 63, 70, 77, 84	0, 7, 14 21, 28, 35 42, 49, 56, 63, 70, 77, 84

ADDITION/MULTIPLICATION 9

1. 0, 0, 0, 0, 0, 0, 0, 0, 0   2. 1, 2, 3, 4, 5, 6, 7, 8, 8

3. 2, 4, 6, 8, 10, 12, 14, 16, 16   4. 3, 6, 9, 12, 15, 18, 21, 24, 24

5. 4, 8, 12, 16, 20, 24, 28, 32, 32   6. 5, 10, 15, 20, 25, 30, 35, 40, 40

7. 6, 12, 18, 24, 30, 36, 42, 48, 48   8. 7, 14, 21, 28, 35, 42, 49, 56, 56

9. 8, 16, 24, 32, 40, 48, 56, 64, 64   10. 9, 18, 27, 36, 45, 54, 63, 72, 72

11. 10, 20, 30, 40, 50, 60, 70, 80, 80

12. 11, 22, 33, 44, 55, 66, 77, 88, 88

13. 12, 24, 36, 48, 60, 72, 84, 96, 96

0, 8, 16 24, 32, 40 48, 56, 64, 72, 80, 88, 96	0, 8, 16 24, 32, 40 48, 56, 64, 72, 80, 88, 96
0, 8, 16 24, 32, 40 48, 56, 64, 72, 80, 88, 96	0, 8, 16 24, 32, 40 48, 56, 64, 72, 80, 88, 96

ADDITION/MULTIPLICATION 10

1. 0, 0, 0, 0, 0, 0, 0, 0, 0, 0
2. 1, 2, 3, 4, 5, 6, 7, 8, 9, 9
3. 2, 4, 6, 8, 10, 12, 14, 16, 18, 18
4. 3, 6, 9, 12, 15, 18, 21, 24, 27, 27
5. 4, 8, 12, 16, 20, 24, 28, 32, 36, 36
6. 5, 10, 15, 20, 25, 30, 35, 40, 45, 45
7. 6, 12, 18, 24, 30, 36, 42, 48, 54, 54
8. 7, 14, 21, 28, 35, 42, 49, 54, 63, 63
9. 8, 16, 24, 32, 40, 48, 56, 64, 72, 72
10. 9, 18, 27, 36, 45, 54, 63, 72, 81, 81
11. 10, 20, 30, 40, 50, 60, 70, 80, 90, 90
12. 11, 22, 33, 44, 55, 66, 77, 88, 99, 99
13. 12, 24, 36, 48, 60, 72, 84, 96, 108, 108

0, 9, 18 27, 36, 45 54, 63, 72, 81, 90, 99 108	0, 9, 18 27, 36, 45 54, 63, 72, 81, 90, 99 108
0, 9, 18 27, 36, 45 54, 63, 72, 81, 90, 99, 108	0, 9, 18 27, 36, 45 54, 63, 72, 81, 90, 99 108

ADDITION/MULTIPLICATION 11

1. 0, 0, 0, 0, 0, 0, 0, 0, 0, 0, 0
2. 1, 2, 3, 4, 5, 6, 7, 8, 9, 10, 10
3. 2, 4, 6, 8, 10, 12, 14, 16, 18, 20, 20
4. 3, 6, 9, 12, 15, 18, 21, 24, 27, 30, 30
5. 4, 8, 12, 16, 20, 24, 28, 32, 36, 40, 40
6. 5, 10, 15, 20, 25, 30, 35, 40, 45, 50, 50
7. 6, 12, 18, 24, 30, 36, 42, 48, 54, 60, 60
8. 7, 14, 21, 28, 35, 42, 49, 54, 63, 70, 70
9. 8, 16, 24, 32, 40, 48, 56, 64, 72, 80, 80
10. 9, 18, 27, 36, 45, 54, 63, 72, 81, 90, 90
11. 10, 20, 30, 40, 50, 60, 70, 80, 80, 100, 100
12. 11, 22, 33, 44, 55, 66, 77, 88, 99, 110, 110
13. 12, 24, 36, 48, 60, 72, 84, 96, 108, 120, 120

0, 10 20, 30 40, 50 60, 70 80, 90, 100, 110, 120	0, 10 20, 30 40, 50 60, 70 80, 90, 100, 110, 120
0, 10 20, 30 40, 50 60, 70 80, 90, 100, 110, 120	0, 10 20, 30 40, 50 60, 70 80, 90, 100, 110, 120

ADDITION/MULTIPLICATION 12

1. 0, 0, 0, 0, 0, 0, 0, 0, 0, 0, 0, 0
2. 1, 2, 3, 4, 5, 6, 7, 8, 9, 10, 11, 11
3. 2, 4, 6, 8, 10, 12, 14, 16, 18, 20, 22, 22
4. 3, 6, 9, 12, 15, 18, 21, 24, 27, 30, 33, 33
5. 4, 8, 12, 16, 20, 24, 28, 32, 36, 40, 44, 44
6. 5, 10, 15, 20, 25, 30, 35, 40, 45, 50, 55, 55
7. 6, 12, 18, 24, 32, 36, 42, 48, 54, 60, 66, 66
8. 7, 14, 21, 28, 35, 42, 49, 56, 63, 70, 77, 77
9. 8, 16, 24, 32, 40, 48, 56, 64, 72, 80, 88, 88
10. 9, 18, 27, 36, 45, 54, 63, 72, 81, 90, 99, 99
11. 10, 20, 30, 40, 50, 60, 70, 80, 90, 100, 110, 110
12. 11, 22, 33, 44, 55, 66, 77, 88, 99, 110, 121, 121
13. 12, 24, 36, 48, 60, 72, 84, 96, 108, 120, 132, 132

0, 11 22, 33 44, 55 66, 77, 88, 99 110, 121 132	0, 11 22, 33 44, 55 66, 77, 88, 99 110, 121, 132
0, 11 22, 33 44, 55 66, 77, 88, 99 110, 121, 132	0, 11 22, 33 44, 55 66, 77, 88, 99 110, 121, 132

ADDITION/MULTIPLICATION 13

1. 0, 0, 0, 0, 0, 0, 0, 0, 0, 0, 0, 0, 0
2. 1, 2, 3, 4, 5, 6, 7, 8, 9, 10, 11, 12, 12
3. 2, 4, 6, 8, 10, 12, 14, 16, 18, 20, 22, 24, 24
4. 3, 6, 9, 12, 15, 18, 21, 24, 27, 30, 33, 36, 36
5. 4, 6, 12, 16, 20, 24, 28, 32, 36, 40, 44, 48, 48
6. 5, 10, 15, 20, 25, 30, 35, 40, 45, 50, 55, 60, 60
7. 6, 12, 18, 24, 30, 36, 42, 48, 54, 60, 66, 72, 72
8. 7, 14, 21, 28, 35, 42, 49, 56, 63, 70, 77, 84, 84
9. 8, 16, 24, 32, 40, 48, 56, 64, 72, 80, 88, 96, 96
10. 9, 18, 27, 36, 45, 54, 63, 72, 81, 90, 99, 108, 108
11. 10, 20, 30, 40, 50, 60, 70, 80, 90, 100, 110, 120, 120
12. 11, 22, 33, 44, 55, 66, 77, 88, 99, 110, 121, 132, 132
13. 12, 24, 36, 48, 60, 72, 84, 96, 108, 120, 132, 144, 144

0, 12, 24, 36 48, 60, 72, 84, 96, 108, 120, 132, 144	0, 12, 24, 36, 48, 60, 72, 84, 96, 108, 120, 132, 144
0, 12, 24, 36, 48, 60, 72, 84, 96, 108 120, 132, 144	0, 12, 24, 36, 48, 60, 72, 84, 96, 108 120, 132, 144

DIVISION 1

1. 8 2 0 4 9 8   2. 0 6 9 2 7 11   3. 7 6 6 3 10 3   4. 3 3 6 0 4 4
5. 5 8 12 5 11 7   6. 6 7 9 9 6 5   7. 3 5 10 5 11 4   8. 8 7 9 7 3 8
9. 0 7 8 7 2 10   10. 2 5 9 8 11 10   11. 10 4 5 4 7 10
12. 2 2 9 5 7 9

DIVISION 2

1. 2, 84, 42
2. 1. estimate, guess 2. multiply 3. multiply 4. check
3. quotient, divisor
4. 34   32   21   42   20
5. 55   10   10   92   13
6. 71   71   63   61   40

DIVISION 3

1. 3, ~~48, 24~~
2. 3, 2 13, 71
1. estimate/guess
2. multiply
3. subtract
4. bring down
5. estimate/guess
6. multiply
7. subtract
8. check
3. quotient, divisor, remainder.
4. 74 50 91 61 41
5. 51 r. 292 r. 130 r.
6 93 r. 1 60 r. 2
6. 81 r. 2 50 r. 1 90 r. 4 51 r. 2 30 r. 8

DIVISION 4

1. 5, 240, 48
2. 1. estimate/guess, 2. multiply
3. subtract
4. bring down
5. estimate/guess
6. multiply
7. subtract   8. bring down 9. estimate 10. multiply
                        11. subtract   12. check
   3. quotient, divisor, remainder.
   1. 114   121   111   104   106 r. 4
   2. 108   228   124   132   109
   3. 30 r. 4   31 r. 1   64 r. 1   40   90 r.2

DIVISION 5

1. 8, 644, 80, 4
2. 1. estimate/guess 2. multiply
3. subtract
4. bring down
5. estimate/guess
6. multiply
7. subtract   8. bring down 9. estimate/guess 10. multiply.
                        11. subtract   12. check
   3. quotient, divisor, remainder.
   1. 91 r. 2   50 r. 1   141 r. 3   50 r.
   2. 61 r. 2   2. 61 r. 1   20 r. 5   70 r. 2   42 r. 1   80 r. 1
   3. 70 r. 3   50 r. 2   72 r. 2   90 r. 3 70

ODD NUMBERS

	3		7		11		15	17	
21		25		29		33	35		
41	43	45	47		51	53		57	
	63	65	67	69	71		75	77	
81	83		87	89	91	93	95	97	99
	103	105	107	109		113	115	117	
121	123	125		129	131	133		137	
141		145	147		151	153	155		
	163	165	167	169	171		175	177	
181	183	185	187	189	191	193	195	197	

EVEN NUMBERS

x2	x4	x6	x8	x10
x12	x14	x16	x18	x20
x22	x24	x26	x28	x30
x32	x34	x36	x38	x40
x42	x44	x46	x48	x50
x52	x54	x56	x58	x60
x62	x64	x66	x68	x70
x72	x74	x76	x78	x80
x82	x84	x86	x88	x90
x92	x94	x96	x98	x100
x102	x104	x106	x108	x110
x112	x114	x116	x118	x120
x122	x124	x126	x128	x130
x132	x134	x136	x138	x140
x142	x144	x146	x148	x150
x152	x154	x156	x158	x160
x162	x164	x166	x168	x170
x172	x174	x176	x178	x180
x182	x184	x186	x188	x190
x192	x194	x196	x198	x200

NUMBER SENTENCES 1

1.	2	.3.
$11 + 7 = 7 + 11$	$5 + 10 = 9 + 6$	$12 + 8 = 20 - 0$
4.	5	. 6.
$17 - 10 = 5 + 2$	$25 - 24 = 15 - 14$	$33 + 10 = 20 + 2$
7.	8.	9.
$13 - 9 = 0 + 4$	$16 - 8 = 10 - 2$	$18 - 8 = 8 + 2$
10	11	12.
$24 + 15 = 20 + 19$	$17 + 17 = 17 - 17$	$66 - 26 = 66 + 26$

NUMBER SENTENCES 2

(1)
a. 2
b. 3
c. 4
d. 7

(2)
a. 5
b. 1
c. 2
d. 6

(3)
a. 15
b. 1
c. 12
d. 0

(4)
a. 2
b. 10
c. 2
d. 9

(5)
a. 12
b. 5
c. 7
d. 4

(6)
a. 7
b. 13
c. 5
d. 6

(7)
a. 16
b. 1
c. 19
d. 3,6

(8)

d. 72 x 132 = (9 x 8) x (11 x 11)

(9)

c. 52 - 48 = (9 x 6) – (4 x 12)

PLACE VALUE 1/NUMBER SENSE

	H Th	T Th	Th	H	T	O
1					1	2
2		1	6	0	5	7
3						9
4	2	4	6	6	8	0
5			1	3	0	5
6				1	0	0
7				2	7	2
8					4	0
9				5	0	5
10			3	7	0	8

10. 100   11. 350   12. 920   13. 804   14. 2,000   15. 9,300   16. 4,500
17. 6,660   18. 10,704

ODD NUMERALS	EVEN NUMERALS
25 17 99 3 9	4 66 4 50 22

Least to the greatest.
109, 205, 243, 764, 793, 829, 850, 905, 1,629, 32,601

PLACE VALUE 2

A. one hundred trillion

B. forty-five trillion, seventy-three billion, six million, one hundred ninety thousand, three hundred thirty-three

C. two trillion, nine hundred billion, seven hundred seventy-three million, four hundred thousand, four hundred five

D. three hundred sixty-two billion, ninety million, six hundred eighty thousand, one hundred

E seventy billion. eight hundred five million, ten thousand, ninety

F. five billion, one hundred forty-six million, nine hundred thirty-two thousand, eight hundred seventy

G. nine hundred three million, ten thousand, six hundred nine

H. eighty-five million, fifty-one thousand, ten

I. one million, one hundred two thousand, three hundred six

J. five hundred thousand

K. twenty-five thousand, six hundred four

L. three thousand, nine hundred ninety

M. four hundred ten

1. 345,678   2. 4,350,000   3. 1,909,110,280

SUBTRACTING WITH REGROUPING (ZEROES) I

1. 2	78	23	54	85	66	49	17
2. 5	36	4	27	28	1	9	12

SUBTRACTING WITH REGROUPING (ZEROES) II

1. 108	349	446	235	3
2. 521	712	139	407	264
3. 898	609	195	141	286
4. 41	194	172	779	219
5. 299	166	33	408	555
6. 477	584	221	149	95

SUBTRACTING WITH REGROUPING (ZEROES) III

1. 744	4,210	5,529	950	5,996
2. 1,950	4,654	1,730	3,191	5,988
3. 5,532	1,867	1,201	5	538

SUBTRACTING WITH REGROUPING (ZEROES) IV

1. 21,464	13,151	66,436	32,435
2. 45,050	20,133	24,511	15,678
3. 219,889	356,267	419,248	203,889
4. 389,096	213,982	99,941	199,999

SUBTRACTING WITH REGROUPING (ZEROES) V

1. 4	498	275	459	1,125
2. 4,325	6,677	10,992	49,889	
3. 44,571	71,643	9,202	789,994	
4. 539,957	629,368	812,511	214,445	
5. 458,322	338,898	63,901	165,918	

FRACTION PRACTICE

1. A fraction is a numeral that represents equal parts of a whole.

2. A proper fraction is a fraction whose numerator is smaller than the denominator.

3. Any 5 fractions whose numerators are smaller than their denominators are acceptable such as 1/2, 2/5, 3/4, 5/6, 7/9.

4. An improper fraction is a fraction whose numerator is larger than the denominator.

5. Any 5 fractions whose numerators are larger than their denominators are acceptable such as 5/2, 7/3, 9/5, 4/3, 9/7.

6. A mixed number is a combination of a whole number and a fraction.

7. Any 5 numerals that are a combination of a whole number and a fraction are acceptable.

8. B. equal to   D. the same as

9. 2/8, 3/12, 4/16. 5/20, 6/24, etc. are acceptable answers.

10. I changed 1/4 into equivalent fractions by multiplying the numerator and denominator by the same number.

11. 6/8 = 3/4

12. I reduced or simplified 6/8 by dividing the numerator and the denominator by 2.

13. A. 19/8 B. 39/5 C. 55/8 D. 21/2 E. 7/4

14. I changed the mixed numbers into improper fractions by multiplying the whole number by the denominator and adding the numerator.

14.   Examples: A. 5/2 = 2 ½ B. 7/3 = 2 1/3 C. 9/5 = 1 4/5
D. 4/3 = 1 1/3 E. 9/7 =1 2/7

16. I changed the improper fractions to mixed numbers by dividing the denominators into the numerators. I made the remainder the numerator and the denominator stayed the same.

WRITING THE NAMES OF FRACTIONS

1. three-fourths   2. seven-eighths   3. fifteen-sixths
4. seven and eight-ninths   5. twelve-seventeenths
6. thirty-five and one-half   7. two-thirteenths
8. one-half   9. two-thirds   10. fifty-twenty-fifths

WRITING EQUIVALENT FRACTIONS BY MULTIPLYING 1

1.	2/4	16/18	4/6	8/10	12/14
2.	6/8	6/22	10/12	2/8	4/18
3.	12/21	6/27	9/21	3/9	21/27
4.	9/15	15/21	3/24	12/33	3/18
5.	16/36	4/8	32/36	8/12	16/20

WRITING EQUIVALENT FRACTIONS BY MULTIPLYING 2

1.	12/14	6/8	6/22	10/12	2/8
2.	4/18	8/14	4/18	6/14	2/6
3.	21/27	9/15	15/21	3/24	12/33
4.	3/18	12/27	3/6	24/27	4/6
5.	16/20	24/28	12/16	12/44	20/24
6.	16/28	8/36	12/28	4/12	28/36
7.	20/45	25/35	5/40	20/55	5/30
8.	5/20	10/45	15/25		

WRITING EQUIVALENT FRACTIONS BY DIVIDING 1

1.	½	8/9	1	2/5	2/3
2.	6/7	3/4	3/6	3/8	1
3.	2/9	½	1	1/3	1/3
4.	1/4	1/3	1/4	1/8	1
5.	1/6	4/9	1	½	2/3
6.	½	4/5	1	2/3	1

WRITING EQUIVALENT FRACTIONS BY DIVIDING 2

1. 5/6	1/4	2/9	1	1/11
2. 3/7	1	7/9	3/5	5/7
3. 1/8	1/11	1/6	4/9	1
4. ½	8/9	2/3	4/5	1
5. 7/9	1/6	5/6	1	2/9
6. 4/7				

Five fractions that cannot be reduced or simplified. 4/9, 1/5, 3/7, 5/6, 3/4 or any others that cannot be simplified.

CHANGING IMPROPER FRACTIONS TO MIXED NUMBERS

1. 4	2. 5	3. 2 2/5	4. 2 1/3
5. 1 3/7	6. 3 1/8	7. 2	8. 3 6/10 = 3 3/5
9. 7 1/7	10. 2 1/6	11. 7 ½	12. 3 ½
13. 3 4/6 = 3 2/3		14. 1 1/8	15. 10

CHANGING MIXED NUMBERS TO IMPROPER FRACTIONS

1. 5/2	2. 27/4	3. 15/2	4. 23/6
5. 74/7	6. 53/9	7. 149/12	8. 39/8
9. 5/3	10. 129/5	11. 65/9	12. 58/5
13. 102/6	14. 306/9	15. 257/10	

ADDING FRACTIONS WITH LIKE DENOMINATORS

1. 3/4	2. 5/7	3. 7/10	4. 7/8	5. 10/13	6. 2/3
7. 1/4	8. 1/3	9. 2/5	10. 1/3	11. 1/3	12. 2/3
13. ½	14. 5/6	15. 2/3	16. 1 2/5	17. 1 1/11	18. 1 3/4
19. 1 4/13	20. 1 3/11	21. 1	22. 2	23. 23/25	24. 4/5

SUBTRACTING FRACTIONS WITH LIKE DENOMINATORS

1. 1/4	2. ½	3. ½	4. 5/9	5. 1/4	6. 5/7
7. 7/13	8. 2/5	9. 5/8	10. 1/7	11. 7/11	12. 1/9
13.3/10	14. 5/13	15. ½	16. 2/3	17. 1/7	18. ½
19. ½	20. 1/6	21. 2/3	22. 1/8	23. 3/5	24. 1/5

ADDING FRACTIONS WITH UNLIKE DENOMINATORS 1

1. 1	2. 1	3. 1	4. 8/9	5. 7/16	6. 13/14
7. 8/13	8. 7/20	9. 1	10. ½	11. 1/3	12. 11/27
13. 5/7	14. 12/13	15. 1/3	16. 1	17. 2/3	18. ½
19. 2	20. 3/4	21. 34/39	22. 1/3	23. 3/4	24. 5/6
25. 1 3/14					

ADDING FRACTIONS WITH UNLIKE DENOMINATORS 2

1. 1 1/6	2. 11/14	3. 9/10	4. 1 1/5	5. 1 7/18	6. 11/15
7. 1 5/7	8. 34/35	9. 1 4/45	10. 1 7/30	11. 1 1/18	12. 3/4
13. 2	14. 1 1/4	15. 19/21	16. 1 1/6	17. 1 8/9	18. 11/30
19. 25/28	20. 7/10	21. 1 3/10	22. 11/12	23. 1 7/20	24. 5/9
25. 1 2/3					

ADDING AND SUBTRACTING FRACTIONS WITH LIKE AND UNLIKE DENOMINATORS

1. 1	2. 1 8/21	3. 13/15	4. 1	5. 10/13
6. 10 7/10	7. 8 2/3	8. 17 1/6	9. 40 8/11	10. 4 13/18
11. 3/7	12. 7/12	13. 1/3	14. 2/13	15. 3/5
16. 8	17. 6½	18. 30 4/21	19. 50 2/5	20. 7 1/3

MULTIPLYING FRACTIONS AND MIXED NUMBERS

1. 1/3	2. 3/8	3. 2/15	4. 3/10	5. 4/21
6. 1/6	7. 1/10	8. 3/10	9. 3/16	10. 1/4
11. 1/6	12. 3/14	13. 1/5	14. 1/10	15. 1/4
16. ½	17. 2/15	18. 3/5	19. 3/10	20. 2/5
21. 12 1/4	22. 4 9/10	23. 12 5/6	24. 18	25. 56

DIVIDING FRACTIONS AND MIXED NUMBERS

1. 1 ½	2. 1 1/3	3. 1 3/5	4. 1	5. 2
6. 2	7. 8	8. 1 2/5	9. 1 3/4	10. 3 1/3
11. 1 1/8	12. 1 19/30	13. 5/6	14. 3 1/5	15. 1 5/16
16. 2 1/4	17. 1 1/5	18. 8/9	19. 1 4/21	20. 5/9
21. 1	22. 2	23. 1 9/10	24. 2 8/9	25. 1 1/3

WRITING DECIMAL NAMES

1. four   2. twenty-four   3. one hundred fifty-five   4. two tenths
5. seven tenths   6. six and nine tenths   7. fifteen hundredths
8. seventy-five hundredths   9. seven hundredths
10. three and nine hundredths   11. two hundred thirty-eight thousandths
12. sixty-seven thousandths   13. one thousandth
14. three and eight hundred one thousandths
15. two hundred forty-five and one tenth

ADDING AND SUBTRACTING DECIMALS

1. 1032	2. 738	3. 1.40	4. 10.47	5. .419
6. 1421.22	7. 546	8. 701	9. 20,551	10. 6.4
11. 717.06		12. 94.634		

MULTIPLYING DECIMALS

1. 31.5   2. 12.22   3. 4.5933   4. 18.5818   5. 78.246   6. 3.12390

DIVIDING DECIMALS BY WHOLE NUMBERS AND DECIMALS

1. .6   2. 7.1   3. 125.01   4. .4439   5. 71.17   6. 2.67
7. .5   8. 5.1   9. 7.25   10. 270.2   11. 257   12. .26

DECIMAL/FRACTION REVIEW

1.   .400
   39.000
   + 6.370
      .001
   45.771

2. 300.23
   - 1.26
   298.97

3. 17,250
5. 1, 2, 4, 8
1, 2, 4, 5, 10, 20
1, 2, 3, 4, 6, 9, 12, 18, 36

4. 78 R.26
1, 13
1, 5, 7, 35

6. 4/6   numerator -- 4   denominator -- 6

$$\frac{4\div2}{6\div2} = \frac{2}{3}$$

6a.   6/4 numerator -- 6   denominator -- 4
             6/4 = 1 2/4 = 1½

7. 3/4 = 6/8 $\frac{3 \times 2}{4 \times 2} = \frac{6}{8}$

8. 1/3 + 2/3 = 3/3 = 1   9. 2/5 + 3/10 = 7/10   10. 11/12

FRACTIONS, DECIMALS, PER CENTS

Fractions	Decimals	Percentages
½	0.5	50%
1/3	0.33	33%
1/4	0.25	25%
1/5	0.20	20%
3/4	0.75	75%
1/10	0.1	10%
2/3	0.66	66%
1 1/4	0.125	125%
4/5	0.80	80%
7/20	0.35	35%
3/20	0.15	15%
25/5	5.	500%
4/4	1.	100%

MEASURING TIME

1. 7   2. 5   3. 4
4. September, April, June, November   30 days
January, March, May, July, August, October, December   31 days
February 28 days 29 days
5. 365   6. 366,4   7. 52   8. 12   9. 10
10. 20   11. 100   12. 1,000

UNITS OF DISTANCE

1. 12 in.	2. 36 in.	3. 3 ft.	4. 36 in.
5. 72 in.	6. 96 in.	7. 9 ft.	8. 24 ft.
9. 36 in.	10. 72 in.	11. 7 yds.	12. 4 yds.
13. 15 ft.	14. 42 ft.	15. 9 ft.	16. 36 in.
17. 21 ft.	18. 108 in.	19. 6 yds.	20. 33 ft.
21. 27 ft.	22. 60 in.	23. 84 in.	24. 9 yds.
25. 18 ft.	26. 5 yds.	27. 3 yds.	28. 30 ft.

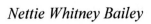

III SOCIAL STUDIES (GEOGRAPHY)

STATES IN THE UNITED STATES OF AMERICA Group I (1)

Alabama, Alaska, Arizona, Arkansas
California, Colorado, Connecticut
Delaware
Florida
Georgia

STATES IN THE UNITED STATES OF AMERICA Group II (2)

Hawaii
Idaho, Illinois, Indiana, Iowa
Kansas, Kentucky
Louisiana
Maine, Maryland, Massachusetts, Michigan, Minnesota, Mississippi,
Missouri, Montana

STATES IN THE UNITED STATES OF AMERICA Group III (3)

Nebraska, Nevada, New Hampshire, New Jersey, New Mexico, New
York, North Carolina, North Dakota
Ohio, Oklahoma, Oregon
Pennsylvania
Rhode Island
South Carolina, South Dakota,

STATES IN THE UNITED STATES OF AMERICA Group IV (4)

Tennessee, Texas
Utah
Vermont, Virginia
Washington, West Virginia, Wisconsin, Wyoming

CONTINENTS

1. North America, Canada, Mexico, United States of America
2. Antarctica 3. Australia   4. Africa   5. Asia
6. Europe   7. South America
2, 4, 7, 5, 6, 3

ABOUT THE AUTHOR

Nettie Whitney Bailey is the youngest of five children born during the depression on Chicago's westside to parents who were community-minded educators.

After becoming a wife and mother of three, she returned to school with the support of her husband and earned undergraduate and graduate degrees in education from Chicago Teachers College and Northwestern University, respectively.

As a retired tutor for Chicago Public Schools, a private tutor in her home, and an educational consultant for DePaul University, all from her bed or wheelchair, she continues to see what teachers and students need.